PROPHETS :

THEIR LIVES & TIMES

Moses, Jesus, Muhammed, Raam & Budh

By

Hari D. Sharma, Ph.D.

authorHOUSE

1663 LIBERTY DRIVE, SUITE 200
BLOOMINGTON, INDIANA 47403
(800) 839-8640
www.authorhouse.com

First published by AuthorHouse 04/29/04

ISBN: 1-4184-1253-8 (e)
ISBN: 1-4184-1254-6 (sc)

Library of Congress Control Number: 2004091125

Printed in the United States of America
Bloomington, Indiana

This book is printed on acid-free paper.

Dedicated To

My wife Jaya Sharma
And our children
Samir & Lena Sharma
For their patience and support

Contents

PREFACE

This book presents the lives and times of the five spiritual giants that human history has ever known. They have influenced a significant majority of the human race through many centuries. Their influence has not only been in the spiritual field, but they also have provided religious, social, and political leadership to humanity. Numerous individuals, over many centuries, have dedicated their lives in the service of humanity by following the paths outlined by these great men of vision. They all led their followers by showing them the righteous path which they practiced themselves i.e. they were leaders who led by personal examples.

These five leaders were: (1) Moses, who led Jews out of slavery and made them into a great nation. He also laid the theological foundation that gave laws to Jews and to later great religions: Christianity and Islam. (2) Jesus, who preached to Christians about the righteous path. He also guided them towards a pure life and died for their sins. (3) Muhammad, who led Muslims away from idol worship. He fought for their rights and also gave laws to Muslims through revelations from God. (4) Raam, who fought for the freedom of worship for all, irrespective of their ways of worship. He also lived with the poor and the weaker section of the society, understood their problems and worked for their equal rights. His personal life, as an ideal man, has been the guiding light for Hindus. (5) Budh, who preached the path to human salvation to his followers. He spread the message of Dhammapada (the path to righteousness), which is followed by Budhists. He has also motivated millions, who have been the followers of other religions, as well.

The chapter on **Moses,** first discusses about his ancestors and their history of migration to Egypt. This is then followed by the information on his birth and marriage, how he was commanded by God to bring Israelites out of Egypt, his encounters with Pharaoh and Exodus from Egypt. Subsequently, forty years of wandering including revelation of the Ten Commandments, his trials and tribulations during the period of wandering, and his last years are presented. Finally, with an overview and Moses' gift to humanity, the chapter on Moses is concluded.

The chapter on **Jesus** begins with a brief background of the Israelite society of his time, his genealogy and birth, baptism and the temptation of Jesus. This is followed by discussions on his reformist preaching, teachings, miracles and healing of the sick and the handicaps. The information on Jesus' entry into Jerusalem, his confrontation with the corrupt establishment, his arrest, crucifixion, burial and resurrection are then presented. After presenting the information on his pious and dedicated life, an overview of his spiritual life and his gift to the humanity are outlined.

The chapter on **Muhammad's** life and time begins with the description of social, economic and political conditions in Arabia prior to and at the time of his birth. This is followed by discussions on his life and experiences in Mecca, including various revelations, preaching, oppositions and his migration from Mecca to Medina. During his stay in Medina, he had many revelations that resulted into social reforms and his strong opposition to idol worship. It also was the place where he made many treaties, established organizations and won battles against his distracters. Finally, his establishment of Muslim community, an overview of his life's achievements and gift to humanity are presented.

The chapter on **Raam**, begins with the background information on the social and the religious environment in the Indian subcontinent at the time of his birth. It has also been mentioned that, unlike other societies, in India, there has always been a kind of separation of the state and the church; for which he fought hard to retain. This is followed by the information on his birth, education, apprenticeship and marriage. Information on his fighting for the freedom of worship, helping and teaching the poor and the social outcasts and defeating the evil power, is presented. The chapter concludes with an overview of his life-long sacrifices and a summary of his gifts to humanity.

The last chapter of this book deals with the life and time of **Budh** which begins with a discussion on the theological, social and political environment in the part of India where Budh was born. This is followed by the information on his birth, marriage and renunciation with the goal to search the truth about human life, suffering and the way to attain peace and happiness. Information on his life, during the period of his meditation and learning, his achieving enlightenment, establishment of his church and preaching are then discussed. Finally, an overview followed by a summary of Budh's gifts to the humanity, are presented in this chapter.

The author was born and raised in a society where Hindus, Budhists, Muslims and Christians have lived, for centuries, as neighbors. He grew up in an environment where young people of different faiths spent their younger days playing together, going to their houses as friends and learning and celebrating one another's religious festivals and getting familiarized with different ways of worship. This was followed by his coming to North America, about thirty five years ago, to pursue his graduate work. This provided him a wonderful opportunity of being exposed to another multi-cultural, multi-religious, a freer and a progressive society. In this free environment, the author further learnt and experienced the Christian and the Jewish faiths. All this experience was complimented by his reading various scriptures, thinking and comparing the teachings of the Prophets and concluding that all Prophets had one goal: leading the humanity to the righteous path as instructed to them by the Almighty God. These Prophets were born in different societies and at different times. But they all basically had the same messages; as expressed in Sanskrit: *Loka Samsta Sukhino Bhawanto, Vasudhav Kukumbakam and Om Shanti, Shanti and Shanti ;* meaning: May Everyone in the Entire World be Happy, The Entire world is One Family and May There Be Peace, Peace and Peace. Realization of this basic truth has resulted in the conception and creation of this book.

Many thoughts, ideas and facts presented in this book are the ideas also propagated by   many scholars whose works the author has either read or has heard them over the years. Identifying and remembering the specifics of each of these thoughts is difficult; their contributions in providing a maturity in the author's thinking are respectfully acknowledged. Documents which have been used directly for this book are referenced at the end of the book and their contribution is thankfully acknowledged.

Hari D. Sharma, Ph.D.

1

INTRODUCTION

Since time immemorial, we humans have wondered about our origin: where did we come from? Why do we die and where will we go after death? What will happen to us once we die? Above all, almost on a daily basis, we have wondered about: Why do things happen to us the way they do? On some occasions there does appear to be an explanation for what happens to us by using the "cause and effect" theory related to our actions. However, in many other situations this does not appear to apply. We seem to be punished when we think that we did not do anything wrong and on the other hand, sometimes we appear to be rewarded unexpectedly. The question is: Why?

When our ancestors throughout the ages, in every society, contemplated about all these issues they tried to establish a relationship between our deeds and the consequences. When the results of all that happens to us could not be explained the "fate" of an individual was the reason given to such unexpected reward or punishment system. On the other hand, some people began explaining all these consequences by saying that there is a supernatural power that is watching us and is making decisions, for each individual, about these rewards and punishments based on a certain set of rules. Consequently, humans began worshiping such power(s) so as to be on the right side of such an omnipotent deciding power.

As human civilization developed, religious, social and political leaders emerged in each society. These leaders were men with vision, leadership qualities and prophetic powers. These Prophets presented the answers to various questions raised by the masses about their lives and what was happening to them on a daily basis. They also presented a set of "dos and don'ts". This book has attempted to present the lives and times of five Prophets: Moses, Jesus, Muhammad, Raam and Budh. These Prophets have influenced and have guided a vast majority of human race through many centuries. These five great men of their time are the Prophets of the present day major religions; Raam is for Hindus, Moses is for Jews, Christians and Muslims, Budh is for Buddhists, Jesus is for Christians and Muhammad is for Muslims.

Presenting the lives and times of such great men is very difficult and is a monumental task. There is an extensive list of biographical and historical literature on the lives of these individual Prophets. Among the various scholarly works on this topic, there appear to be many variations in these presentations. For example, in some instances the events are presented differently and in other cases they are interpreted differently, each providing their convincing and supportive arguments and evidences. All this has made it a difficult task in presenting a definitive document on their lives and time. Actually it appeared that a large amount of the scholarly work on the lives and times of these Prophets, reviewed by the author, actually is about the Judaism, Christianity, Islam, Hinduism and the Budhism, as the writers interpreted, but not about the Prophets. After reviewing various books on the subject related to Moses, Jesus, Muhammad and Raam, the author decided to primarily rely on the information provided in The Living Torah, Bible (Good News: New Testament and Psalms), The Glorious Qur'an, and Shri Ramcharitmanasa. For Budh, the author obtained information from Dhammapada, and earlier sections of Buddhism and The Spirit of Buddhism. Additional information was obtained from a few pertinent sections of some more texts on the topic. These are listed in the reference section at the end of the book.

Information on Moses was primarily obtained from the Torah. The details were obtained from the "The Five Books of Moses", consisting of Genesis, Exodus, Leviticus, Numbers and Deuteronomy. The information on Jesus was compiled from the gospel consisting of The Gospel according to Matthew, Mark, Luke and John. For Muhammad, the information was primarily obtained from the Introduction to The Glorious Qur'an and the 114 Surahs of Qur'an. Information on the life and time of Raam was obtained from the seven chapters of Ramcharitmanasa: Balakanda, Ayodhyakanda, Aranyakanda, Kishkindhakanda, Sundarakanda, Lankakanda and Uttarakanda. Finally, information on Budh was obtained from the Dhammapada (sayings of Budh), Buddhism: the Light of Asia and The Spirit of Buddhism.

As shown in Figure 1.1, all the five Prophets, whose lives and times are presented in this book, were born in the region that lies within the bounds of latitude approximately between 10 degrees and 35 degrees north and longitude approximately between 30 degrees and 90 degrees east; a very limited geographical zone mostly consisting of warm to hot climatic conditions. Chronological dating for the period of these Prophets is not well defined and scholars still have difficulty in identifying the exact dates; older the time period of a Prophet is, the more difficult it becomes to identify a date for his birth time period. Therefore, the dates cited here are for general understanding of the century when these Prophets were born. At this time, it is generally, believed that Raam was born in and around 2000 B.C, Moses was born in and around 1200 B.C., Budh was born in and around 560 B.C., Jesus was born in and around between 1 B.C. and 1 A.D. and Muhammad was born in and around 570 A.D.

As will be exhibited in the following chapters, all these Prophets preached about the God and for the welfare of the entire human race. Although they were born many centuries apart and preached in areas that were many hundreds and, in some cases, many thousands miles apart, their messages were basically similar. They preached for one God and for the basic human rights.

With the author's humble and respectful bow to these great Prophets, the following chapters present the times and lives of these great men who have been the guiding lights for humanity through the ages.

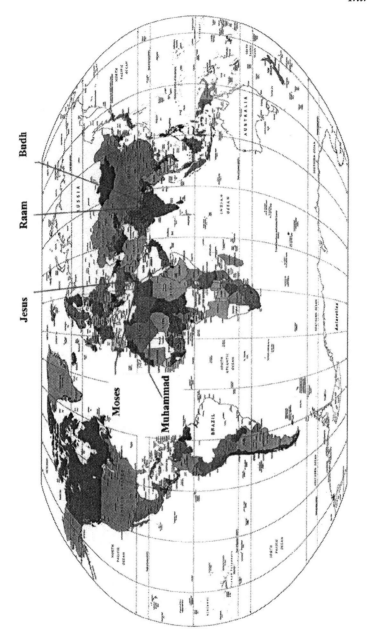

Figure 1.1 The Geographical Regions Where the Five Prophets Were Born
(Base Map: Courtesy of The General Libraries UT at Austin, 2003)

2

MOSES

2.1 MOSES' ANCESTORS MIGRATING TO EGYPT

Adam to Abram (later named Abraham)

According to Genesis the beginning started with God creating heaven and earth followed by light and darkness, day and night, water and dry land, plants and trees, flying creatures and sea monsters, species of live stocks and beasts and finally God created man. All the creation was completed in six days. On the seventh day, God stopped all the work that He was doing and declared the **seventh day to be holy**.

Man was created out of dust of the ground. God placed man in the Garden of Eden which translated in English means the garden of delight. God's first commandment to man was: do not eat "from the Tree of Knowledge of good and evil". Man was told that the day he will eat from this tree he will die. From man's rib God made woman. The woman saw that the Tree of Knowledge in the Garden was attractive and was good to eat from.

Therefore she ate some of its fruit and gave some to the man who also ate it. Because man, who was named Adam, did not follow God's commandment He banished both Adam and his wife Eve from the garden and took away their immortality i.e., they both will, one day, die.

Thus the first generation of man was Adam followed by his son Seth. Of the chronicles of Adam his eighteenth generation grandson was Terach who fathered Abram, Nachor and Haran. Terach left Ur Cardin with his son Abram, his grandson Lot (who was Haran's son) and Abram's wife Sarah and headed towards the land of Canaan. However, they came as far as Charan, a city in Mesopotamia, and settled there. According to Rabbi Kaplan, the journey from Ur to Charan was approximately 600 miles and Charan was about 400 miles northeast of the Holy Land (Figure 2.1).

Abraham's Migration and Off springs

According to the book of Genesis 12:1, **God said to Abram "Go away from-----your birth place -------to the land I will show you". God also promised to Abram that He will make him into a great nation**. Abram did as God had directed him. He was 75 years old when Abram left Charan. His wife Sarah, his nephew Lot, his servants and his spiritual followers accompanied him as he headed towards the land of Canaan. Abram traveled as south as the area in the vicinity of present day Nablus- a city named Shechem near the center of Holy Land as identified by Rabbi Kaplan (1981). God appeared to Abram and said, **"I will give this land to your off springs"** (Genesis 12:7). Abram then moved on to the mountain east of Bethel, a city north of Jerusalem; he set up a tent there and built an altar there. Abram traveled south to Egypt since there was a famine in the land and stayed in Egypt for a while since famine had grown severe in the land of Canaan (see Figure 2.1 for Abraham's journey: as suggested by Kaplan, 1981).

In Egypt, Abram acquired wealth. He became very rich with silver, gold and livestock. With all his wealth Abram headed north until he came back to a place near Bethel and set up his tent. Abram then lived in the land of Canaan. In the land he had to fight to keep his land and wealth. After **Abram** had lived in Canaan for 10 years and he was 86 years old, he

had a son born from his wife's slave-girl Hagar who he named **Ishmael**. When Abram was 99 years old, God appeared to him and said that he **must circumcise every male** when the male is eight days old. God also said to Abram that henceforth his name will be **Abraham** and his wife's name will become **Sarah**. At that time Abraham, his son Ishmael and all men of his household and slaves were circumcised. When Abraham was 100 years old his wife Sarah gave birth to their son named **Isaac**. **Abraham** married another woman who bore him six children. At the end of his life, Abraham gave all he had to his son Isaac.

Isaac married Rebecca and had twins named Esau and Jacob. Isaac settled in Gerar. Isaac farmed the area and with time became extremely wealthy with flocks of sheep, herd of cattle and a large number of slaves. The Philistines became jealous of Isaac. Therefore, their King Abimelekh said to Isaac to leave the area because he felt that Isaac had become too much more powerful than he was and realized that Isaac could be a threat to him. Isaac, therefore, left the area and then tried to settle at a few locations by digging wells for water in those places. Finally, he settled in Beer-Sheba where he also found sufficient amount of water for his use. God appeared to Isaac and blessed him. Isaac built an altar there in God's name.

Isaac had grown old and his eye sight was fading when Rebecca manipulated him in such a way that Isaac ended up giving all he had to his younger son Jacob although originally he had intended to give this to his older son Esau, the first born. This made Esau angry and consequently he planned to kill Jacob. Rebecca came to know of this plan and advised Jacob to flee to her brother Laban in Charan. Rebecca did not like Esau because he had married Judith daughter of Beeri, the Hittite. Knowing this, Isaac also asked Jacob to go to Padan Aram and marry a daughter of his maternal uncle Laban. In view of this Jacob went to Charan. There he married Laban's two daughters Leah and Rachel. Both Leah and Rachel each also gave their respective handmaids to Jacob as his wives. With his hard work and management skills, with time, Jacob became very wealthy. He acquired many sheep, goats, camels and donkeys, as well as slaves. Jacob then asked his father-in –law Laban to let him take his wives, children and a fair share of his wealth and let him go to his own land Canaan. Laban did not agree to his proposal.

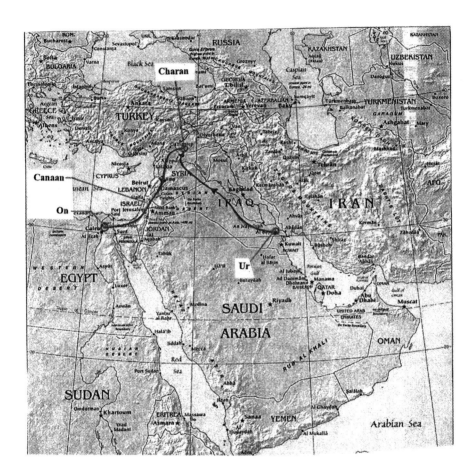

Figure 2.1 Abraham's Journey
(Base Map: Courtesy of The General Libraries UT at Austin, 2003)

Exodus of Jacob (later named Israel) from Charan (in the land of Padan Aram) to the Land of Canaan

God said to Jacob, "Go back to your birth place in the land of your fathers. I will be with you" (Genesis 31:3). Jacob, therefore, prepared for the travel to see his father Isaac in the land of Canaan. He started his journey by packing his goods he had acquired, putting his children and wives on the camels and heading away with all his livestock. Actually, Jacob did not tell his father-in-law that he was leaving. Once Laban knew that Jacob had fled he along with his kinsmen, pursued Jacob for seven days until Laban caught up with Jacob. Laban then asked Jacob the reason for his leaving. He also said to Jacob that he could do a great harm to him but would not do so since God was with him. Jacob and Laban then both made peace with one another and both then went their ways- Jacob to the land of Canaan and Laban back to the land of Padan Aram.

Jacob then continued his journey but was still afraid of his brother Esau. Jacob, therefore, sent messengers to his brother Esau, along with selected tribute of goats, sheep, camels, cows, bulls and donkeys. Esau returned all gifts back to Jacob and welcomed him with love and affection.

Now that Jacob had returned to Canaan, God appeared to him and said, "----your name will not be only **Jacob; you will also have Israel as a name**" (Genesis 35:10). Jacob settled in the area his father had lived. With his four wives Jacob had twelve sons. His favorite wife Rachel was the mother of his **youngest sons Joseph and Benjamin**.

Joseph Sold: His trials and Tribulations

Since Joseph was Israel's child of his old age he loved him more than his other sons. This made Joseph's older brothers hate him. Once Israel asked Joseph to go to Shechem, where his brothers were keeping the sheep, and see how his brothers were doing and then return to Israel with the information of their well being. When Joseph's brothers saw him coming, they began plotting to kill him. After a brief argument among themselves, they decided to throw him into a well, which turned out to be dry. After a while the brothers saw an Arab Caravan that had loaded camels with gum, balsam and resin headed for Egypt. Judah, one of Joseph's brothers, suggested that instead of killing their own brother they should sell Joseph to Arabs. This, he added, will serve two purposes (i) they will not have to bear the curse of killing their own brother and at the same time (ii) Joseph will be sent away from their home. To this, they all agreed and sold Joseph to Arabs for twenty pieces of silver. The Arabs later sold Joseph in Egypt to one of Pharaoh's officers.

As time passed, Joseph worked hard and smart thus gaining favor with his master who eventually appointed him as his personal servant. Joseph grew up to be a handsome young man. He caught favor in his master's wife's eyes who eventually asked Joseph to sleep with her; Joseph refused to this proposal. In retaliation, she charged him with an attempted rape; resulting in Joseph's arrest and imprisonment.

Pharaoh's two courtiers, the wine steward and the baker, offended their master and were also sent to the same prison where Joseph was serving his time. One night each of the two imprisoned courtiers had a dream. In the morning when Joseph saw them upset, he asked them the reason for their distress. In response, each related to Joseph their respective dream; Joseph then interpreted their dreams. The interpretation was that the wine steward's job will be restored but the baker will be put to death. As Joseph had predicted, on the third day which was Pharaoh's birthday, the chief steward's job was restored but the chief baker was put to death.

After two years, Pharaoh had two dreams. In the first dream, he saw that as he was standing near the Nile seven healthy looking fat cows emerged from the Nile. Then he saw another set of seven ugly looking cows emerging from the Nile. The seven lean looking cows ate up the seven fat cows. In the second dream, Pharaoh saw seven fat ears of grain growing on a single stalk. He then saw that the seven thin ears of grain that grew behind the fat ears of grain swallowed up the seven fat ears.

Next morning, Pharaoh was very unhappy. He narrated his dreams to all courtiers and wise men but no one could provide a satisfactory interpretation of his dreams. Eventually, the chief wine steward recalled his experience in the prison and related Joseph's ability to interpret the dreams correctly. Pharaoh sent messengers and Joseph was brought in to him. After hearing Pharaoh's dream, Joseph presented the interpretation as follows:

Joseph said that God was telling Pharaoh that seven fat cows and good healthy looking ears of grain were seven good years of plenty, while the seven lean cows and the seven thin ears of grain represented seven years of famine that will follow the years of surplus in Egypt. In view of this, Pharaoh should place a man, with insight and wisdom, in-charge of collecting and managing food surplus during seven good years and then distributing them to the needy during the famine years.

Joseph's Rise to the Position of Viceroy in Egypt

After hearing the dream interpretations, Pharaoh said to Joseph that since God chose him to provide such an important information to the king he was the one who should have wisdom and insight to perform such a task. Pharaoh then made Joseph the viceroy and gave him authority over entire Egypt. Joseph was also given Asenath, daughter of the priest of On (the center of worship of sun-God Ra), as a wife. Joseph was 30 years old when he was made viceroy. Joseph had two sons born to his wife Asenath.

Joseph toured the entire land of Egypt and made arrangements to collect and store wisely during the seven years of abundance. At the end of these seven years of surplus, seven years of famine began. When people appealed to Pharaoh for bread he announced to all Egyptian people to go to Joseph and follow his instructions. Joseph helped people by appropriately rationing out the food collected, in his stores, during the good years. Joseph's rationing out the food was like a dictator. In other words, he was the only one who would ration out food to people; thus cutting out the middle man.

As famine spread over the entire area, Jacob (also called Israel) heard that food supplies were available in Egypt. Therefore, he sent his ten sons (Joseph was eleventh and Benjamin the twelfth and the youngest son) to buy grain in Egypt. When Israel's ten sons approached Joseph for food they prostrated themselves to him and did not recognize him. Joseph, however, recognized them but did not reveal his identity. He accused them of spying on Egypt. They humbly responded by saying that they are twelve brothers, sons of Israel, from Canaan. They continued by saying that the youngest one was with their father and one was gone. Joseph told them that nine of them should go and get the youngest one. In the mean time, one of them was to be kept there under arrest as a hostage. They agreed to such an arrangement. When they returned to their father with supplies and the message that Benjamin should come with them to Egypt, at first Jacob refused to comply. As they consumed the supplies they had obtained from Egypt, Jacob asked his sons to get more food from Egypt. They refused to go without Benjamin, because they feared that without their youngest brother they all will be killed on reaching Egypt. Finally, Israel relented and let Benjamin go with his brothers.

When Joseph saw his brother Benjamin, he was filled with emotions. He first welcomed them all and treated them well and served them good meals. At first though, for a while he also gave them tough time but eventually revealed his identity. He also told his brothers that he now was Pharaoh's vizier. Hearing this, they all broke down and wept loudly. Joseph told them not to feel guilty and also wept so loudly that even Egyptians heard him. This news eventually reached Pharaoh. Pharaoh instructed Joseph to instruct his brothers to take wagons from Egypt and bring their children, wives and father. He told them to come back to Egypt and assured them that on their return all things would be provided for them. Back in Canaan, before starting his journey, Israel offered sacrifices to God. **God** spoke to Israel in a night vision and **said, "------go to Egypt, for it is there that I will make you a great nation"** (Genesis 45:3). Jacob came to Egypt with his all children and their families; in total they were seventy.

Israel's Descendents Settle in Egypt and Prosper

Joseph told Pharaoh that his father's family had arrived from Canaan. He also said that they had come with their sheep and cattle and their profession was to deal with livestock and they were also tenders of sheep. Pharaoh responded by letting them settle in Goshen district, the best area for the purpose. **With time Israel's descendents lived and prospered in Egypt,** in the Goshen district. Accordingly, their population grew rapidly. On Israel's death, his body was embalmed; this was similar to a custom that was prevalent in Egypt at that time.

Joseph lived to be 110 years old. At the time of his death, Joseph told Israelites that when God grants them providence, they must take his remains to the promise land. On his death Joseph was also embalmed and placed in an ornamental stone coffin.

According to Exodus 1:7, "the Israelites were fertile and prolific, and their population increased. They became so numerous that the land was filled with them." This gave the people of Israel a great power. As time passed and through many generations, they also acquired Egyptian or other local ethnic customs, language and social practices. However, since a majority of them settled in a certain part of the country, they also retained a large part of their identity.

2.2 BIRTH AND EARLY YEARS OF MOSES

Many years had passed after Joseph's death. During this period Israelite's population grew significantly. Their numbers became so large that they dominated the area they had settled. Consequently their influence also grew far and beyond.

A new kingdom or dynasty of Egyptian origin had come to power. This started with Ach-Moshe, who drove a Semitic tribe called Hyksos, out of Egypt. Hyksos' main power lied in a north-east Nile delta city of Pithom (Tanis): which was the chief commercial center of Egypt (Kaplan, 1981). Although Israelites were not expelled, their Semitic origin put them in the list of suspicious people. The new regime thought that since Israelites were increasing in numbers and becoming strong, in the event of a war they may join the enemies of the state. The entire Israelite population was thus perceived as a political and economic threat to the Egyptian Kingdom.

In order to check this threat, Egyptian King executed a two prong strategy. First, conscription officers were appointed over Israelites, who were put to hard labor involving bricks and mortar and build cities like Pithom and Ra'amses. Second, all male infant babies were to be killed by casting them into the Nile. The first action was intended to break their spirits and the second was aimed at reducing their population.

Moses : Birth to Marriage

In Egypt, the sons of Levi were Gershon, Kehoth and Merari (Number 3:17). Kehoth's one of the sons was Amram whose wife's name was Yokheved- also a daughter of Levi family. Yokheved bore three children to Amram; their names were Aaron, Moses and their older sister Miriam (number 26:59). Moses was the youngest one and was three years younger than Aaron.

From Adam to Moses the chronology was as follows:
- **Adam-Eve** had son **Seth**
- Eighteenth generation grandson of Adam was **Terach**
- Son of Terach was **Abraham**
- Abraham had two sons: **Ishmael and Isaac**
- Isaac had twins: Esau and **Jacob**
- Jacob also called Israel had 12 sons; **Joseph** and Benjamin were the youngest ones
- Joseph helped Israelites settle in Egypt
- After many generations of Israelites in Egypt, one of the descendents of Levi family of the Israelite community had three sons: Gershon, **Kehoth** and Merari
- Kehoth's one of the son's was **Amram**
- Amram had three children: Miriam, Aaron and **Moses**

Moses' mother kept him hidden for three months after his birth. When it became impossible for her to keep her infant hidden, she prepared a paprus box and coated it with asphalt like red clay. This made it a water-tight floating basket or box. Yokheved then placed her young child, Moses, in the box and placed the box in the uncut paprus near the Nile River's bank. She then instructed her daughter, Miriam, to stand at a distance and watch "what would happen" to the child.

When Pharaoh's daughter went to take a bath in the river Nile, she saw the box in the uncut paprus. She then sent her slave-maid to bring the box back to her. After opening the box the princess, Pharaoh's daughter, saw the infant boy who began crying. Seeing this, the princess had pity on the infant. After looking at the child, she realized that it was a Hebrew boy. The child's older sister, Miriam, who was watching this, came near and asked if she should call a Hebrew woman to nurse the child for the princess. Pharaoh's daughter replied in affirmative. Miriam went and got her (or child's) mother, Yokheved. The princess asked Yokheved to take the child and nurse him and paid her a fee for the service. The woman nursed the child and returned him to the princess when the child was two years old. The princess then adopted the child and named him Moses (or Moshe), which meant a son or also meant drawn from water.

As Moses was growing up he saw the hard labor his fellow Hebrew were being subjected to. **One day he saw an Egyptian kill one of the Hebrews. This incident changed the course of his life. As a punishment to this murder, Moses killed the Egyptian**. He then hid the dead body in the sand. A fellow Hebrew man had seen Moses kill the Egyptian. Next day he told this to Moses. Hearing this Moses became fearful of its consequences. Once Pharaoh heard of this murder, he "took steps to have Moses put to death". **Moses fled to the land of Midian,** about 250 miles east of Memphis. Incidentally, one should note that it is the same Midian whose Arab (Midianite Arab) had first bought and then sold Joseph, many generations, earlier to Egyptians. Now the people of the same place were giving shelter to one of Joseph's descendants, Moses.

One day when Moses was sitting near a well he saw seven girls, who were daughters of a local Sheik, drawing water and trying to water their father's sheep. Other shepherds attempted to chase these girls away. Moses came to these girls' help and, in turn, chased all these shepherds away. He then watered Sheik's sheep. When the girls returned home, they related the story to their father. Hearing this, the sheik asked the girls to bring the stranger to their home. **Moses came and lived with them and eventually married Sheik's daughter Tzipporah (which means lady-bird). They together had a son named Gershom.**

Moses the Reluctant Leader: receives his Marching orders

Moses lived in his father-in-law's home, with his family, for a long time and tended his sheep. He would go places with sheep and would migrate to different areas suitable for grazing and water. Moses, once, led his flock to the Horeb area; this area was in and around Sinai. This area was very dry. **When Moses was in this area, tending his sheep, he saw a fire in the middle of thorn-brush.** Moses looked at it and was surprised to see that, although the brush was on fire, it was not consuming the brush. As curious Moses began moving towards the fire, he heard God's voice calling his name, "Moses, Moses". Moses replied in affirmative. **God then said to Moses that** He had seen the suffering and pain of Israelites in Egypt. God continued and said that **He " will bring them out of that land, to a good, spacious land, to a land flowing with milk and honey, the territory of the Canaanites, Hittites, Amorites, Perizzites, Hivites and Yebusites"** **(Exodus 3:8).**

Moses, at this stage, was doubtful of his abilities for the job of bringing Israelites out of Egypt. Because of this he asked the question to God: how would Israelites believe him that he had been sent by God to bring them out of Egypt and lead them to the Promised Land? God responded by saying that Moses should go to Egypt and gather the elders of Israel and tell them that "God of Abraham, Isaac and Jacob" had appeared to him and had instructed him to lead the people of Israel out of Egypt. God continued by saying, "they will take what you say seriously". God also told Moses that he and the elders of Israelites will then go to the King of Egypt to communicate God's order. It was also revealed to Moses that the King of Egypt will not allow Moses to lead His people out of the land until the king, at a later time, will be forced to do so. "I will then display My power and demolish Egypt through all the miraculous deeds that I will perform in their land. Then Pharaoh will let you leave" (Exodus 3:20). Moses then replied that he will have a great difficulty in convincing people that God had appeared to him and had told him about leading Israelites out of Egypt. Hearing this, God asked Moses to throw his staff on the ground; which he did as God had instructed him. The staff turned into a snake. God then asked Moses to grasp its tail. As soon as Moses did that the snake turned back into the staff. **God then showed a second miracle to Moses** by asking him to put his hand on his chest. When Moses complied with God's instruction, his hand became leprous. Then God asked him to place it back into his robe and then remove it. On removing his hand from the robe, the leprous looking hand turned normal. God then told Moses that if Pharaoh still did not believe all this then "you shall take some water from Nile and spill it on ground". The water will turn into blood. Moses then pleaded to God by saying that since he was not a good speaker he would not be able to convince people by his words. God then replied by saying that **Aaron, his brother, was a good speaker and from now on he will be Moses' spokesman while Moses will be his guide. God continued by saying "Take this staff in your hand. With it, you will perform the miracles"** (Exodus 4:17).

From now on, Moses became a man of ideas, God's messenger and the leader while Aaron became the communicator or the spokesman.

Moses Accepts Leadership Role and Prepares His People to Leave Egypt

As time passed, the King of Egypt died and a new Pharaoh came to power. The Israelites were still being put to subjugation under the new Pharaoh, as was the case under the previous regime.

Moses left Midian, his father-in-law's place, with his wife, two sons and his divine staff. He then set out to return to Egypt. On the way he met his brother Aaron and told him about his mission, as God had commanded him, as well as the miraculous proof that God had provided him. Aaron related all this to Israelites; they all accepted this.

Moses and Aaron then went to Pharaoh and told him that God had instructed them to ask Pharaoh to let Israelites leave Egypt. In response, the King told them that they should continue doing their own businesses and should not distract people from their work. Moses then exhibited the miracles of his staff to Pharaoh, as God had told him to do. Pharaoh did not pay attention to this.

2.3 ENCOUNTERS WITH PHARAOH AND EXODUS FROM EGYPT

Encounters between Moses and Pharaoh and Nine Plagues

First, as God had told Moses, Aaron extended the staff over the waters of Egypt. The consequence was that **all waters** (rivers, streams, canals, and other water storage areas) **were transformed into blood**. This resulted in the death of fish in the Nile and water became so polluted that Egyptians could no longer drink the Nile's water. This remained so for seven days. In spite of seeing all this from his own eyes Pharaoh did not pay attention to this sever trouble. **Second,** Aaron held his hand over the waters of Egypt and all **areas were covered with frogs.** Seeing this Pharaoh asked Moses and Aaron to pray to God so that all the frogs leave. He then promised that if Moses did this then he will let his people leave Egypt. Moses prayed and all frogs left houses and other places and went into the Nile. After seeing this, Pharaoh refused to honor his commitment, as God had predicted earlier.

Third, at God's instructions through Moses, Aaron held out his staff and struck the dust of earth. This **turned lice all over Egypt.** Pharaoh still would not let Israelites leave. **Fourth,** Moses told Pharaoh to let his people leave otherwise the **entire ground will be filled with harmful creatures.** Pharaoh still would not listen. Therefore the entire land of Egypt was filled with these harmful creatures. Seeing this pharaoh again asked Moses to pray to his God to rid the land from the creatures. Moses complied with the request. But Pharaoh still did not let his people leave Egypt. **Fifth,** God **killed all livestock** belonging to Egyptians; the Israelites livestock was not harmed. Still Pharaoh would not listen. **Sixth,** Moses and Aaron threw furnace ash into the air. **This caused rashes and boils on men and beasts** in Egypt. Pharaoh still did not listen.

The **seventh** plague hit Egypt as God **caused thunder, hail and lightening that killed all outdoors men, creatures, plants and trees**. Again, Pharaoh requested to Moses and Aaron to pray to God to stop all this. Moses agreed and prayed to God. This resulted in that all the hail and the lightening stopped. But Pharaoh, as before, did not honor his words. Then God caused the **eighth plague by bringing the locust invasion on Egypt**. Pharaoh again asked Moses and Aaron to pray to God and remove the locust invasion; they did so. Consequently, the land became free from locust but Pharaoh still did not relent.

God caused the **ninth plague by asking Moses to lift his hand towards the sky; this caused darkness all over Egypt for three days**. Pharaoh summoned Moses, asked him to worship his God. In return he said that he would allow his people and their children leave Egypt. However, he said that they will not be allowed to take their sheep and cattle with them. Moses refused to accept this offer.

Passover and Tenth and the Final Plague

God told Moses that "there will be one more plague". Moses was told that the plague will be so destructive to Egyptians that Pharaoh will let Israelites leave. Therefore, Moses was instructed by God to prepare his people for the departure- **Exodus** (see Figure 2.2 for the route; as suggested by Kaplan, 1981).

In response to God's command, Moses summoned the elders of Israel and asked them to gather the people and instruct them to get sheep for Passover sacrifice. One animal was sacrificed by each family and the sacrificial blood was then put over the beams and the door posts. All people were asked to stay in door over the entire night.

In the night time, God passed over all the houses and killed every first-born in Egypt. God, however, spared houses that belonged to Israelites; these houses were marked by Passover sacrificial blood on their door posts. Experiencing such a mass destruction and weakened by previous plagues, Pharaoh summoned Moses and Aaron and ordered them to leave Egypt with all their people, their families, sheep, cattle and all belongings. As instructed by Moses, Israelites requested silver and gold articles and clothing from Egyptians who promptly granted their request. "The Israelites thus drained Egypt of its wealth" (Exodus 12:36). The Israelites left Egypt with about 600,000 adult males with their families, sheep, cattle, livestock and belongings. It is also generally agreed that a great mixture of nationalities left with them; the group is estimated to be over a million people. This ended about 430 years of stay of Israelites in Egypt. Moses also took Joseph's remains with him to further reinforce in Israelites mind that even Joseph, who was responsible for Israelites' settlement in Egypt, was with them.

Figure 2.2 The Exodus Route
(Base Map: Courtesy of The General Libraries UT at Austin, 2003)

2.4 FORMATION OF A NATION : WANDERING YEARS

Israelites Leave and Egyptian Forces Pursue Them

The shortest route from Egypt to the promise land was through the Philistine Highway, which was along the Mediterranean coast and passed through Philistine territory. Since there was ancient enmity between the Philistines and the Israelites, Moses chose a longer path through the desert to the Red sea so as to avoid armed resistance from the Philistines. Moses and his people were not prepared for such a battle. Any loss or even a fight would have discouraged the Israelites and there was a possibility that they might have returned back to Egypt. So the selection of a longer and more difficult desert route was a strategic decision.

When Pharaoh saw so much of his manpower and wealth leaving Egypt, he decided to stop them. He summoned his military leaders and organized a force to pursue Israelites who were leaving the land. As Israelites saw Pharaoh's chariots, cavalry and infantry they became fearful of being captured, persecuted and killed. **Under the panic mode they began blaming Moses for their ill fate. Moses spoke to them with confidence and advised them to have faith in God.** He told them to stand firm, be silent, have faith and God will rescue them. Moses then prayed to God. God spoke to Moses and told him to raise his staff and extend his arm. As Moses followed God's instructions powerful winds blew that transformed the sea bed into dry land. Israelites then entered the dry land. Egyptian army gave Israelites a chase. However, Israelites moved very fast and crossed the area when the winds had parted the sea and had made it a dry land. Egyptian army was not so fast in their pursuit. **As the winds subsided, the waters came back drowning Pharaoh's entire army.** After having such a life saving experience, **Israelites "believed in God and his servant Moses".** All Israelites then sang and danced in praise of God.

People Travel and Face Further Difficulties: Faith Building

Moses then led his people into the desert away from the Red sea. They traveled through the desert **without finding any water** and when they found water it was bitter. When people complained to Moses, he prayed to God. God showed Moses a certain tree and told him to throw it into the water; Moses complied with God's order and the water became drinkable. Actually, Moses and his people had now learnt one of the desert survival techniques. It also instilled in them that if they followed God's commandments they will be rewarded.

The entire Israelite community then continued camping and traveling. On the fifteenth day of the second month after leaving Egypt, in the desert, **people started complaining about the shortage of food.** When Moses prayed to God, God through Moses and Aaron told the entire community that in the afternoon they will eat meat and in the morning they will have bread. As God had promised, "that evening, a flock of quail came and covered the camp". In the morning, "there were little grains all over the surface of the desert". Moses told the Israelites that it was the bread that God, as promised, had given them to eat- one Omer (a measure equal to around two quarts) was assigned for each person. When Friday came, Moses told Israelites that what they will gather that day will be double in amount since it had to be both for Friday and Saturday. Moses said that there will be no food gathering on Saturday- the Sabbath day: the day of rest. So work was to be done during the six days and **the seventh day was announced to be Sabbath- a day of rest and religious dedication.**

They then traveled through the desert until the community camped in Rephidim, some ten miles west of Mount Sinai. They again encountered water scarcity resulting in quarrel with Moses; they began demonstrating against him. God instructed Moses that he take the people along with the elders to the rock of Horeb. He was then told to strike the rock with his staff. As Moses did this, water came out of the rock. At this camp, Amalek, **a tribe descended from Esau, Isaac's son, attacked Israelites.** Moses told Joshua to engage Amalek in the battle while he, Aaron and Chur (an important leader with Aaron of the tribe of Judah) went up to the top of the hill and held his hands up; thus providing guidance and encouragement to the troops. **By sunset Amalek and his allies were defeated in the battle. This reaffirmed Israelites faith in God and Moses.**

Selection of Capable People for Administration and Delegation

Jethro, Moses' father-in-law who was Sheik of Midian, brought to Moses his wife, who had been sent home earlier, and her two sons- Gershom and Eliezer. Moses then related to Jethro all what had happened to Pharaoh and how God had rescued Israelites through difficult times. The next day Moses' father-in-law saw how Moses was involved in helping people from morning to evening and how busy he was in solving their problems. In light of this, he advised Moses that this situation was not good. He told Moses that if he kept on helping people alone, pretty soon he would wear him out. Jethro suggested that **Moses should set up an organization consisting of capable and God-fearing men as leaders**: "leaders of thousands, leaders of hundreds, leaders of fifties and leaders of tens". He continued by saying that **these leaders should then administer justice to people**. Moses agreed with his advice. All these appointed men administered most of the justice and only difficult cases were brought to Moses' attention. Thus, a justice system was established by Moses on the advice of his father-in-law, who then left for his homeland.

The Ten Commandments: Difficulties and Final Acceptance

As Israelites traveled, they arrived in the Sinai Desert and camped opposite to the Mount Sinai. Moses meditated and went up to God. God then told Moses to remind the people what good things He had done to them because they obeyed Him in the past. God continued by saying that if they kept His covenant they all will be His beloved and chosen people among all nations. Moses then came back to the elders and the people and told them what God had said. On hearing this, the people of Israel agreed to accept and follow God's commands. Then God gave instructions to Moses to sanctify people and tell them to stay at the bottom of the mountain and not to cross a boundary around the base of the mountain.

God then came down on the peak of Mount Sinai and summoned Moses there. God then spoke by saying the following words:
1. **I am God your Lord.** (This is a commandment stating that people must believe in God).
2. **Do not have** (or make or represent) **any other God before Me.**
3. **Do not take the name of God in vain.** (This prohibits false oaths and unnecessary use of God's name).
4. **Saturday is Sabbath to God your Lord. Do not do any work on Sabbath day.**
5. **Honor your father and mother.**
6. **Do not commit murder.**
7. **Do not commit adultery.**
8. **Do not steal.**
9. **Do not testify as a false witness against your neighbor.**
10. **Do not be envious of your neighbor's house.** (This also includes neighbor's wife, his slaves and all that your neighbor has).

After God spoke, all Israelites saw flames and smoke in the mountain and also heard sounds and the blast of the ram's horn. Seeing and hearing all this all people got frightened. God had exhibited this so that they fear God and do not sin.

Following this many other laws were enunciated so that an orderly society can be established. These laws were related to: offering limitations, buying and freeing slaves, maidservants, manslaughter, kidnapping, idolatry and oppression, lending money, accepting authority and many others (Exodus 20:19 through 23:33).

After finishing what God had to say to Moses, He gave Moses two stone tablets of the Testimony. Since Moses was away so long on the Mount Sinai, people became concerned about his well being. They went to Aaron and asked him to make a deity that will answer their questions especially about what happened to Moses. Aaron asked them to bring gold to him; they complied with the instructions. Aaron took the gold and had someone cast it into a calf. When people saw this some of them began saying that this is your god. Then Aaron built an altar before the calf and announced that "tomorrow, there will be a festival to God." Next morning people started making offerings and began eating, drinking and enjoying themselves. Observing this God became angry and directed Moses to go down and tell people to refrain from such evil acts.

Moses descended the mountain with two Tablets in his hand. After seeing the calf and people dancing and celebrating, Moses displayed anger and threw the tablets on the ground thus shattering them into pieces. Moses then took the calf, burnt it into the fire, grounded it into powder, scattered it on the water and made the people drink it. He then ordered that all those who were involved in the idolatry be killed. As Moses had ordered, the Levites followed his directives and killed approximately three thousand people. Moses then went to God and asked for His forgiveness. Moses pleaded to God to forgive His people's sins and lead them to the land He had ordered him to take to. God relented and told Moses to carve two tablets like the first ones, and take them to Mount Sinai next morning. Moses did as God had told him to do. Moses stayed on the mountain with God for forty days and forty nights. During this period, Moses did neither eat bread nor did he drink water. God then wrote the Ten Commandments on the Tablets, just like the first ones.

With the two Tablets of Ten Commandments in his hand, Moses came down from Mount Sinai; when he came down Aaron and all Israelites noticed that Moses' face was shinning with brilliant light. Moses then told Israelites what God had told him. He reiterated that God had told him that if the people followed His Commandments then God will lead them to the Promised Land which is filled with milk and honey. He will drive the Amorites, Canaanites, Hivite, Perizzites, Hittites and Yebusites out of the land. He also told the people that God had instructed that Israelites should not make treaties with those people, do not worship their gods and do not have any relationship with them. To avoid any future God's anger they were also told to follow God's Commandments.

Travel Continued, Other Laws Made and the Census

Moses then told Israelites that God has told him that He has selected Betzalel, of the tribe of Judah, as the architect who will be able to devise plans, work in gold, silver and copper, cut stones, do carpentry and other skilled work. Betzalel and Oholiav, of the tribe of Dan, then taught others these skills. All of the most talented craftsmen then started work on the construction of Tabernacle and in due course completed it. Moses then erected the Communion Tent Tabernacle. Once all the work was done, the cloud covered the Communion Tent and the Tabernacle was filled with God's glory. As the cloud would rise from the Tabernacle, it was signal to Israelites to move on and travel and when the clouds did not rise they would not move on. This signal remained throughout their travels.

As the people of Israel traveled through their journey, other laws were enunciated. Among some of these laws were: laws of (i) offerings, (ii) installation of priests, (iii) dietary laws, (iv) rituals for keeping clean, (v) purification of a leper, (vi) sexual laws, (vii) holiness laws (viii) penalties and rewards. These laws are described in detail in the Book of Leviticus.

Several penalties were established for major crimes that would result in "put to death by stoning" or "burned with fire". Rules were also established for helping others. For example, it was told that if ones brother (whether a proselyte or a native Israelite) becomes impoverished and loses the ability to support himself one must come to his aid and help him to survive.

For being obedient by following His laws and commandments, the rewards were also outlined. These were that God will provide rain at the right time, the land will bear ample food and fruits and He will grant peace in the land. Punishments were described for not following all the commandments. The punishments for disobedience included that there will be food shortage and the people will be defeated by their enemies.

Thus during the entire period of the travel, God through Moses revealed laws and commandments and other social norms to be followed by the Israelites. All this kept them motivated to travel towards their goal, kept deviants out and established a unified society that also helped each other.

On the first day of the second month in the second year of the Exodus in the Sinai Desert, God told Moses to take a census of the Israelite people. Accordingly, Moses took a tally of the community by their tribe. Thus the census of the twelve tribes who were the descendants of: Reuben, Simeon, Gad, Judah, Issachar, Zebulun, Ephraim, Manasseh, Benjamin, Dan, Asher, and Naphtali was taken. The total number for each tribe was then added. The entire tally was 603,550 (Numbers 1:46). This total did not include the Levites who were made in-charge of the Tabernacle of Testimony.

Fire, Hunger, Disease and Even Moses' Siblings Spoke Against Him

As Israelites traveled through hardships their patience started running thin. They began complaining to Moses about their difficulties and began comparing their relatively comfortable living in Egypt which they left behind and agreed to follow Moses. They started questioning their decision and blamed Moses for all this. Hearing this God became angry and exhibited His anger by a **fire** that consumed the edge of the camp. Israelites cried to Moses who then prayed to God for forgiveness. As a consequence the fire died down. A few days after a large number of people started having cravings for meat. They started weeping and demanded meat. They expressed that they were **hungry** for fish, cucumbers, melons, onions, garlic and other food stuff that was easily available in Egypt. But now they had to contend with only the cake made out of manna, a coriander seed looking grain which they were gathering from the ground. Moses turned to God and complained to Him the fate He has given to the people. They were going without meat, fish, fruits and other delicacies for such a long time. God told Moses to go and collect his people. He informed Moses that from next day they will have ample meat for a full month. Next day God caused a wind that swept quails up from the sea. The wind was so strong that so many quails landed on the ground that people had many times more than they needed. They all gathered and ate them more than they needed to. God displayed his anger and struck them with severe **plague**. People who had such cravings died there.

Moses' wife Tzipporah was a dark-skinned Midianite woman. Because of his wife being dark skinned, Moses' **sister** Miriam and his **brother** Aaron started **speaking against him**. Hearing this,God displayed His anger and made Miriam leprous. Seeing this, Moses prayed to God asked Him to heal his sister. God granted Moses' his wish and after seven days of quarantine she was healed. Israelites then packed and moved on until they next camped in the Paran Desert.

Trials and Tribulations of Forty Years of Wandering

On God's instructions, Moses' selected **a team of Israelite leaders**, one man from each tribe, **to explore the Canaanite territory** which God had promised to His people. Moses told them to head north to the Negev and to continue north to the hill country. Their mandate was to find out about the strengths and weaknesses of the people residing in the land they were sent to explore. They were further told to observe how well the cities are fortified and how good the land was from agricultural point of view. In other words, the team was to evaluate the fertility characteristics of the land. As a proof they were also to bring samples of land's fruits.

After a period of forty days, the advance- exploration team returned and reported their findings to Moses, Aaron and the entire Israelite community. They stated that the land, they were sent to explore, was fertile and was indeed flowing with milk and honey. However, they reported that the people residing in the land were strong and aggressive and the cities were very well fortified. All exploratory team members, except two, said that it will be suicidal to go to the land they had seen during their exploratory task. They said that if Israelites tried to invade them it would result in sure defeat. Hearing this, the entire community started weeping and began shouting in grief. They proposed to go back to Egypt where they claimed to have had better and safer lives. People began suggesting that **a new leader be appointed** who can take them back to Egypt.   Only two team members, Joshua of Ephraim tribe and Caleb of Judah tribe, disagreed with them. Both Joshua and Caleb addressed to the entire community and said that the land was really good and was flowing with milk and honey. They continued by strongly stating that people should not rebel against God because He was with them and they will win against those who are residing in that land. The people did not listen to them and threatened them to be stoned to death. Hearing this God became angry and the exploratory team members, except Joshua and Caleb, died of the plague. Seeing this, the Israelites overcame with terrible grief and declared that they will follow God. As a proof, they then picked up their swords and moved towards the top of the mountain. The **Amalekites and Canaanites,** who were living on that mountain **attacked and defeated the Israelites**. God spoke to Moses and said that people have defied Him. God through Moses told the people that their punishment was that they will wander for forty years in the desert until their sin is forgiven and finally their children will succeed in reaching the land promised to them by God.

Korach, a great-grandson of Levi, along with Dathan and Aviram, descendants of Reuben with two hundred fifty Israelites of rank in the community began a **rebellion against Moses and Aaron**. They confronted them by questioning their holiness and not accepting their place above God's congregation. Moses tried to reason with Korach and reminded him that he and all other Levites have already been given privileged place in the community. He said that, in addition to all this, now also demanding the position of priesthood is against God. Moses then summoned Dathan and Aviram. They did not come. All this infuriated Moses. Moses then excommunicated them and told the entire Israelite community to keep away from the rebellious group. They were warned that if they did so they will be punished for their sin. People complied with Moses' instructions. God was so angry with this confrontation that all the people and their houses were swallowed under the ground that split below them. The earth then covered them over. Seeing this, the people began demonstrating against Moses and Aaron. God became angry with this behavior of Israelites. He struck people with plague that killed 14,700 people in addition to people killed earlier with Korach. Experiencing so much of deaths and fearing future punishments, the surviving Israelite community promised to follow Moses and Aaron as God had commanded.

2.5 LAST YEARS OF MOSES

Moses' Siblings Die

The Israelites traveled for thirty nine years. During this period the entire generation of the Exodus had died. Then in the first month, Nissan, of the fortieth year Israelites arrived at the Tzin Desert. The community stopped in Kadesh where Moses' older sister died; she was buried there. Here, people began demonstrating against Moses because there was no water there. Moses first tried to appease the demonstrators. When he did not succeed in satisfying people he prayed to God. On God's instructions Moses and Aaron summoned the community before a cliff. Then, Moses raised his hand and struck the cliff with his staff twice. This resulted in a large amount of water gushing out of the cliff satisfying the thirst of the entire community and their animals.

From Kadesh, Israelites continued their journey until they came to Hor Mountain. When they arrived at the mountain Aaron died on top of the mountain. Aaron's son Eleazar was then vested with the responsibility that was earlier given to Aaron.

Israelites Attacked by Canaanites, confrontation with Sichon and Og And Israelites Punished for their Sins

Arad, the Canaanite king lived in Negev. When he heard that Israelites are traveling along the main highway leading through the Negev toward Beer Sheba he attacked them. They also took some Israelites as captives. Israelites prayed to God and vowed to retaliate. They eventually defeated Canaanites and then moved on. When they came to the borders of the kingdom of Amorites, they sent emissaries to their king Sichon. They asked permission to peacefully pass through their territory. The king refused to give such permission. In retaliation, Israelites struck him down with the sword and occupied his land. They then settled in their towns and cities. Israelites then headed north towards Bashan. King of Bashan, Og, came out and fought a battle with Israelites. Israelites defeated him, killed him and his people and occupied his land.

When Israelites were staying in Shittim they began immoral behavior with Moabite girls. They also started worshipping Moabite Gods and became involved in idol worshiping. This behavior made God angry. God ordered Israel judges to kill all those who were involved in idolatry. After some hesitation culprits were penalized. When it was over 24,000 people had died.

The New Census Taken and Inheritance Rules Established

As commanded by God, Moses and the new priest Eleazar (son of late Aaron) summoned the Israelites and told them **to count** all males over 20 years of age and are fit for duty. Tally of Reubenite families was 43,730, families of Simeon was 22,200, Gad's descendants were 40,500, Judah's families numbered at 76,500, and the families of Issachar were 64,300, Zebulun were 60,500, Manassehs were 52,700, Ephraims were 32,500, Benjamins were 45,600, Dan's were 64,400, Ashers were 53,400, and Naphtali families numbered 45,400. When the counting was completed the total tally of the Israelites was 601,730. This number was down by 1820 from the first census which was 603,550.

After the census was completed, the land was divided as an **inheritance** in accordance with the numbers recorded in each groups. Thus, a group with larger number of people was given a larger inheritance and smaller group was given the smaller inheritance. However, irrespective of the group size, the **hereditary** land or the property was given to families or tribes through a lottery system. The hereditary property was to pass over to a person's **son** on his death. However, if a man died without having a son then his property would be given to his **daughter**. Further details of the inheritance law were also decreed as God had commanded to Moses.

Moses Dies

Moses followed God's command and climbed up to the Avarim Mountain. From its top Moses could "see the land that I am giving to the Israelites" (Numbers 27:12). In other words he could "see the land of Canaan that I am giving the Israelites as a holding" (Deuteronomy 32:49). Then as God had commanded, Moses took Joshua, son of Nun, and presented him before the priest, Eleazar, and the entire Israelite community. Moses then laid his hand on Joshua and commissioned him as his successor. Moses then died; he was one hundred and twenty years old. Before Moses died, he had established laws to be followed by a civil society, made people practice those laws, nominated well qualified spiritual, judicial, administrative and military leadership and successfully built a nation.

2.6 OVERVIEW AND MOSES' GIFT TO HUMANITY

Israelites, literally meaning "children of Israel", migrated from the land of Canaan to Egypt many centuries prior to Moses' birth. Joseph, son of Israel (also named Jacob), who because of his talents became the viceroy in Pharaoh's court was instrumental in first inviting and then getting Israelites settled in Egypt. Joseph's grandfather was Isaac and great grandfather was Abraham.

With time Israel's descendents lived, grew in numbers and prospered in Egypt. Over the centuries, the entire community achieved a great political and economic power in Egypt. A large number of them also got socially integrated in the Egyptian society. As time passed, a new regime of Kingdom came to power in Egypt. The king, of this new Kingdom, perceived the entire Israelite community as a threat to his kingdom. To break their spirit and control them, the regime put Israelites to hard labor. Additionally, to keep their number low, the Pharaoh ordered that all new born first male Israelite babies be killed by casting them into the Nile. Therefore, Moses' parents, descendents of Levi family of the Israelite community, were afraid for Moses' life when he was born. In view of this, they first hid him for three months and after that period placed him in a water-proof basket and put the basket in the uncut paprus near the Nile. After finding the infant in the basket, the princess - Pharaoh's daughter, adopted the child and named him Moses.

Thus, Moses, born to Israelite parents was raised as an Egyptian prince. He was well educated, learnt the art of war and became experienced in religious principles and leadership skills. As Moses was growing up he saw the hard labor his fellow men were being subjected to. **He believed in the equality of all humans and equal justice for all.** One day he saw an Egyptian officer kill one of the laborers. Despite of being raised in an aristocratic family and having the ruling class upbringing, he still had compassion for his fellow human being even though the person killed belonged to the labor class. As a punishment to the murder, Moses killed the Egyptian who had murdered the laborer. Fearing the consequence of killing an Egyptian officer, Moses fled to the land of Midian. There he married a daughter of a local sheik. He married in a family which was neither a Hebrew, his birth nationality nor an Egyptian, his adoptive ethnic society. His wife was of dark skin; even his siblings, criticized him for marrying a dark skinned person. **Moses valued a person based on his or her qualities. He neither discriminated based on ones skin color nor the ethnic origin.**

While living in Midian with his father-in-law and his family and tending his sheep, Moses had a lot of time for analyzing his surrounding environment, the state of common man and his value system. He also learnt survival techniques in the desert. He wisely synthesized the experiences of elders, gained over many generations, about gathering food and finding water in dry desert environment. Later, he taught all this to his followers. During his stay in Midian, Moses also contemplated about the creation and the creator, the almighty and omnipotent God. In the end, his spirituality brought him close to God. Moses, once, led his flock to the Horeb area; this area was in and around Sinai. Moses saw a fire in the middle of thorn-brush. Moses looked at it and was surprised to see that, although the brush was on fire, it was not consuming the brush. As curious Moses began moving towards the fire, he heard God's voice calling his name, "Moses, Moses". Moses replied in affirmative. God then said to Moses that He had seen the suffering and pain of Israelites in Egypt. God continued and said that He "will bring them out of that land, to a good, spacious land, to a land flowing with milk and honey". God commanded him to lead His people out of Egypt. Who were His people? These were the people of many nationalities who were being oppressed by Egyptian ruling class.

Moses, first, questioned his ability to lead a group of the oppressed slaves. As he thought more and more about it, his compassion for the weaker section of the society grew stronger. Having strong faith in the Almighty God, he heard from his inner self that he was being called by God to perform his Duty to God. Therefore, he accepted the responsibility; knowing well that the task was difficult and dangerous. All this he accepted because **he believed in personal sacrifices so that he could provide leadership in eliminating human sufferings**.

Once Moses accepted God's command to lead the Israelites out of Egypt, away from slavery, he fully dedicated himself to the mission. Since Moses lacked good communication skills, he convinced Aaron, a great communicator, to join him. They then met Israelite elders, established an organization, took advantage of a period when Pharaoh was weak and finally led the Israelite community out of Egypt. He then led Israelites out of Egypt and kept them motivated for about forty years through thirst, hunger, attacks by invaders, internal revolts and general fatigue of long wandering years. Through a combination of persuasion, rewards, punishments and spiritual indoctrination, Moses kept the Israelite community focused on their goals. He led a life of hardships and spirituality along with his fellow travelers. Thus he led his people by his personal examples. **Moses thus established model codes for an ideal leader**.

Leading, moving, feeding and administering a population of over half a million people was not easy. **Therefore, Moses, through years of experimentation, established an efficient bureaucracy, religious leadership, a judiciary, and inheritance laws**. These were great achievements for that period. Moses died before the Israelites could settle in the promise land. However, he had provided his people the ingredients for building a successful nation.

Most importantly, Moses gave laws, in the form of Ten Commandments, for orderly functioning of a civil society. These laws are as follows:

1. **I am God your Lord.** (This is a commandment stating that people must believe in God).
2. **Do not have** (or make or represent) **any other God before Me.**
3. **Do not take the name of God in vain.** (This prohibits false oaths and unnecessary use of God's name).
4. **Saturday is Sabbath to God your Lord. Do not do any work on Sabbath day.**
5. **Honor your father and mother.**
6. **Do not commit murder.**
7. **Do not commit adultery.**

8. **Do not steal.**
9. **Do not testify as a false witness against your neighbor.**
10. **Do not be envious of your neighbor's house.** (This also includes neighbor's wife, his slaves and all that your neighbor has).

Now, through many centuries both inside and outside the Israelite society, these laws have become the moral foundations for millions of people.

3

JESUS

3.1 JESUS' ANCESTORS AND HIS BIRTH

In Egypt, during Moses' early life Israelites were mostly laborers and were being forced to do hard labor and were provided only food and shelter. Prior to their being put to such hard labor due to the changed political situation, Israelites lived a very prosperous life in Egypt. Many of them led elite lives and held positions of power. They intermarried in Egyptian society, took up their customs and in many ways got integrated in the Egyptian culture. However, during the period Moses was born their fate had already changed for the worse. They became poor and Egyptian ruling class was putting them to hard labor. So when Moses led approximately half a million people, out of Egypt, these people though poor were of multi - ethnic background ranging from Israelites to Arabs to Egyptians. The only commonality among them was that they were an oppressed class and most of them believed in the God of Abraham. Through forty years of wandering Moses gave these people laws and modalities to live a civil society. Moses also established an orderly organization consisting of judges, priests, requirements for a place of worship, offering requirements, rewards and punishment system and prepared the people to fight and prepared them to rule in the land that was promised to them by God. After conquering the land of Canaan, Israelites flourished and lived in their land for centuries. During this period they had great kings like David. The society became culturally, economically and politically mature. As time passed they were attacked and were defeated. Following this they were also exiled to Babylon and ruled by Romans. Actually, during the period Jesus was born, almost entire middle - east was under Roman rule (see **Figure 3.1** for Geographical Area Where Jesus was Born).

With defeats, exile, and foreign rule, the people became inward looking. The general public became poor, the masses suffered with many diseases, the priest class, in general, became rigid in the interpretation and application of the teachings of the scriptures.

The ruling class of the land became self-centered, the masses were being subjected to heavy taxation and the weaker and poorer section of the society was suffering the most. Consequently, the Israelite public started having solace in their past and began questioning their current leadership's ability to lead them out of this situation. The people were looking for the Messiah, whose coming was foretold by Hebrew prophets, to save them from such a miserable state. Such was the economical, political, spiritual and emotional state of the Israelite society when Jesus Christ was born.

Jesus' Ancestors

Jesus Christ was a descendant of David who was a descendent of Abraham (Mathew 1.1 and Luke 3:23 to 3:34). According to the scripture (The New Testament) there were fourteen generations from Abraham to King David. These included Abraham, Isaac, Jacob, Judah to King David who was eleventh descendant of Judah and fourteenth descendant of Abraham; Abraham through Judah are also mentioned in the chapter on Moses under title Moses' Ancestors. From King David to the time Israelites were exiled

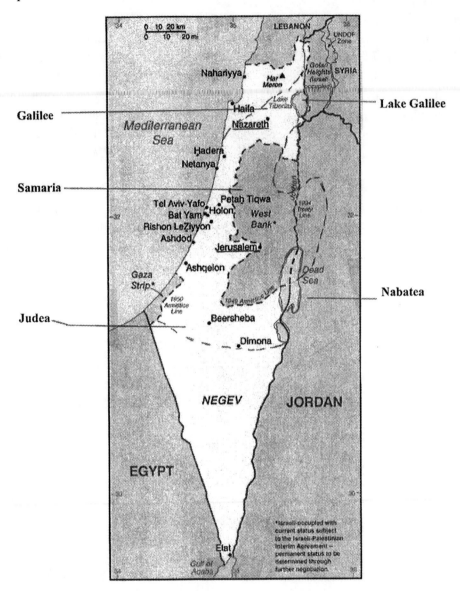

Figure 3.1 The Geographical Area Where Jesus Was Born
(Base Map: Courtesy of The General Libraries UT at Austin, 2003)

in Babylon, the fourteenth descendant of David was Jehoiachin. From the time after the Israelite's exile in Babylon, there was fourteen generations to the birth of Jesus to Mary who was married to Joseph. Thus, Abraham, Isaac and Jacob (later named as Israel) were Jesus' ancestors. They were also the ancestors of Joseph, who invited and settled Israelite people in Egypt and Moses who later brought them out of Egypt many centuries before Jesus was born.

From Adam to Jesus the chronology was as follows:

- Eighteenth generation grandson of **Adam** was **Terach**
- Son of Terach was **Abraham**
- Abraham's son was **Isaac**
- Isaac's son was **Jacob**
- Jacob's son was **Joseph** (he was responsible for getting Israelites settle in Egypt)
- After many generations one of Joseph's descendents in Egypt was **Moses**
- Moses led Israelites out of Egypt to the promise land
- Fourteenth generation grandson of Abraham, in the promise land, was king **David**
- Fourteenth generation grandson of king David was **Jehoiachin**
- Fourteenth generation grandson of Jehoiachin was **Jesus**

Jesus Born

At the time, Mary Jesus' mother, was pregnant with him by the Holy Spirit she was engaged to Joseph who was a descendant of David. When Joseph found out that Mary was going to have a baby, he planned to break the engagement. In the meantime, an angel of the Lord appeared to Joseph in the dream and told him to marry Mary. When Joseph woke up, in accordance with the angel of Lord's instructions, he married her. At that time the Roman Emperor Augustus ordered that a census be taken throughout his empire. Joseph went from the town of Nazareth in Galilee to the town of Bethlehem in Judea, the birthplace of King David, his ancestor, to register. While they were in Bethlehem, the time came for Mary to give birth to her son (Luke 2:6). According to Matthew (1:22 and 1:23) all this happened to make true what the Lord had said through the prophet, "A virgin will become pregnant and will have a son". A week later the baby was circumcised and named Jesus.

Some men, who studied stars, came to Jerusalem from east. They asked about the whereabouts of the baby. They said that they had seen the star in the east and had come to worship the child who they said will be the king of Jews. On hearing about this, King Herod, king of Judea, gave orders to kill all boys, in Bethlehem and its neighborhood, who were two years old and younger (Matthew 2:16). An angel of Lord appeared in dream to Joseph and told him to take the child and his mother to Egypt to protect him from Herod. Joseph followed the instructions of the angel and left for Egypt with Mary and her child. The family stayed in Egypt until Herod died. One can recall that, in the past, Egypt at various times had provided refuse to Abraham, Isaac, Joseph and now Mary and her young baby Jesus.

3.2 RETURN FROM EGYPT, BAPTISM AND TEMPTATION OF JESUS

After King Herod died, Joseph came back to Israel with his wife Mary and her young son Jesus. However, out of fear for young Jesus' life, instead of going back to Bethlehem in Judea where Archelaus had succeeded his father Herod as king of Judea, Joseph went to the province of Galilee. He then made the town of Nazareth, in Galilee, his home.

An interesting instance is narrated in Luke (2: 41 through 2:47) that shows **Jesus' quest for knowledge, interest and understanding of God and Jewish theology even at a tender age of twelve.** As a part of their yearly Passover Festival celebration, Jesus' parents used to go to Jerusalem with Jesus. As during previous years, when Jesus was twelve years old, his parents went to Jerusalem for the Passover Festival. After the festival was over, they traveled back towards their home thinking that their son must be with the children of their relatives and friends in the traveling group. After a day's travel when they found that Jesus was not with the group, they came back to Jerusalem and searched for their son. When they came to the Temple they were astonished to see Jesus "sitting with the Jewish teachers, listening to them and asking questions. All who heard him were amazed at his intelligent answers".

As time passed, Jesus grew up to be a healthy and wise young man. During this period he gained "favor with God and men".

John The Baptist: A Preacher and A Reformer

During the rule of Emperor Tiberius, Pontius Pilate was governor of Judea, Herod was the ruler of Galilee and Annas and Caiaphas were high priests. It was during this time, John the Baptist came to the desert of Judea to preach about God and tell people to turn away from their sins. John's dress code and food choices were different from other preachers. He wore clothes that were made of camel's hair, had leather belt around his waist and ate locusts and wild honey. People liked his preaching so much that they came to him from all over the country near the Jordan River. When people confessed their sins and vowed not to sin in future John baptized them in the Jordan.

Many Pharisees, belonging to a Jewish religious party that believed in strict obeying of the Laws of Moses and other regulations that were added to it through the centuries, came to John for getting baptized. Similarly, many Sadducees who belonged to a small Jewish religious party composed largely of priests also came to be baptized. Actually, Sadducees differed in several matters of beliefs and practice from the larger party of Pharisees; Sadducees based their beliefs primarily on the first five books of the Old Testament. John first rebuked them and then when he became convinced that they had repented and were willing to change by turning away from their sins, he baptized them with water. As John's fame spread around people of various back ground came to him for teachings. For example, when tax collectors came to him to be baptized, he told them, "Do not collect more than is legal." Similarly, when some soldiers came to him, he said, "Do not take money from anyone by force or accuse anyone falsely. Be content with your pay." (Luke : 3:12 through 3:14).

Jesus was impressed with John's teachings and his good work that helped people to follow the right path. He came to John to be baptized by him. John knew that Jesus was a great soul and did not need to be baptized. Therefore, initially John tried to "change his mind". After some discussions, John agreed to baptize Jesus. As soon as Jesus was baptized he was filled with spirituality "and he saw the Spirit of God coming down like a dove and lighting on him".

Temptation of Jesus

Following His baptism and experiencing the vision of the Spirit of God, Jesus was led into the desert by the Spirit to be tested. Jesus spent forty days and nights in the desert without food. When he was very hungry, Devil came to him and said, "If you are God's son, order these stones to turn into bread." Jesus replied that man can not live on bread alone; he also needs spirituality of God. This basically tells that possessing all the material goods can not keep a man satisfied. He needs spirituality as well to keep him happy. Then the devil showed him all the kingdoms of the world and said that if he worshiped the Devil he will be given all the greatness of these kingdoms. Jesus rejected this and strongly stated that he will only worship the Lord our God and no one else. This exhibited Jesus' strong faith in God and also confirmed that he rejected the notion that materialism alone can keep a person happy. Realizing this, the Devil left Jesus alone and stopped tempting him. God's angels then came and helped Jesus.

Jesus Begins His Work.

Because of his open criticism of the corrupt establishment and his ability in successfully convincing people to turn away from their sins, John the Baptist began attracting a large following. This caused resentment among people in power. John was therefore put in prison. Hearing this, Jesus left Nazareth and went to live in Capernaum, a town by Lake Galilee. Jesus began preaching in synagogues. He continued his religious and social reform oriented messages to the masses. His key message was, "**Turn away from your sins, because the Kingdom of heaven is near!**" (Matthew 4:17). The people who came to hear Jesus liked his teachings and they all praised him. With time his fame and good name spread throughout the territory of Galilee.

With time Jesus gained so much of name recognition and fame that once when he was walking along the shore of Lake Galilee he saw two fishermen brothers. Their names were Simon (called Peter) and Andrew. Jesus talked to them and convinced them to follow him to help humanity. They both agreed and went with him. Jesus kept on preaching from place to place and met two other brothers; James and John. They were the sons of another fisherman named Zebedee. Jesus called them; they both left their father and went with Jesus. These were Jesus' first four of the total twelve apostles whom Jesus later chose to be his special followers and helpers. With his four dedicated disciples, Jesus began his work of teaching, preaching and healing the sick.

3.3 JESUS TEACHES AND HEALS

Jesus began his work at the age of thirty years. He traveled all over Galilee and taught in synagogues. As he preached many people with diseases and sickness came to him with great faith. He healed them all. As the news of his good work spread around many people, from different areas, came to hear the good news and to be healed by him.

The Sermon On The Mountain: Jesus Teaches

Large crowds followed Jesus wherever he went. In his sermons and teachings, he used the language of common man. He, therefore, used simple language and parables so that his message reaches the ordinary man on the street. This was unlike many priests who would only have congregation of the elite group of people. Seeing the crowds, Jesus went up a hill and began teaching. Some of his key teachings were as follows:

1. Happiness: Jesus said that true happiness is attained by those who are humble, are merciful to others, work for peace, and are pure in heart.

2. Laws of Moses and Teachings of the Prophets: Jesus emphasized that his teachings do not say that people should do away with these laws and teachings. Jesus said that he was simply explaining them in simple language. He stressed that instead of doing away with the laws people should follow them.

3. Anger Control: Jesus said that in addition to the commandment of "Do not commit murder" one should also get rid of anger. He said that "whoever calls his brother a worthless fool will be in danger of going to the fire of hell." Jesus continued by saying "make peace with your brother."

4. Adultery: Further explanation and extension of the law that states "Do not commit adultery" is that if anyone casts his eyes "at a woman and wants to possess her is guilty of committing adultery."

5. Revenge: Jesus revised the earlier preaching, by others, stating "an eye for an eye, and a tooth for a tooth" to "Do not take revenge." On the contrary he preached forgiveness and said, "If anyone slaps you on the right cheek, let him slap your left cheek too." (Matthew 5:39).

6. Charity: Those who have been blessed with wealth should give something to needy people. However, such charity should not be done publicly. In other words "do not make a big show of it."

7. Prayer: Prayer should be in simple language and should be done in private. Do not make it a big public show "like the hypocrites" do.

8. Judging Others: If you want to be a good person in God's eyes "Do not judge others."

9. Treating Others: Generally people complain about others behavior towards them but do not notice their own behavior. Jesus therefore said, "Do for others what you want them to do for you."

10. False Prophets: Jesus warned people against false prophets. He said be on your guard against them because "they come to you looking like sheep on the outside, but on the inside they are really like wild wolves."

11. Obeying and Practicing These Teachings: Jesus said just hearing the words of his teachings and not obeying them is wrong. He said that obeying and practicing these teachings is like building a house on rock that will stay intact under sever winds, rain and floods.

The crowd was really impressed with Jesus' teachings. He spoke with authority, used common man's language and communicated with conviction. **He taught what he practiced.**

Jesus Heals

Faith healing has been extensively recorded at numerous instances when life of Jesus has been related. After teaching on the mountain, Jesus came down and large crowd followed him. Then **a man with a skin disease** came and requested Jesus to make him clean, i.e. heal him. Jesus said "Be clean". The man was at once cured of his disease. On another instance, in Capernaum, a **Roman officer** asked Jesus to heal his **sick servant** who was home lying in bed. Jesus agreed, and said that he will go to his home and make the servant well. The officer said, "No sir, I do not deserve to have you come into my house." He continued by saying that if Jesus ordered the servant to be cured from there, he was sure that the sick servant will be cured. On hearing this Jesus told his followers how surprised he was seeing that a man from outside Israel had such a great faith; in Israel he did not find people with such firm faith. The officer's sick servant was healed that very moment.

Then Jesus went to Peter's home. There he healed Peter's sick mother-in-law who was in bed with fever. In that evening many people brought many sick people to Jesus and he cured them all. Then according to Matthew (9:1 through 8), Mark (2:1 through 12) and Luke (5:17 through 26) Jesus healed a paralyzed man by forgiving the man's sins. This caused a great uproar among the teachers of the Law who objected Jesus' authority in forgiving ones sins. When Jesus healed a paralyzed man people praised God for giving such an authority to men.

Once, as Jesus was walking along, he saw a tax collector named Matthew. Matthew followed Jesus and invited him for a meal in his house. Many other tax collectors and other outcasts joined Jesus at the table. When some Pharisees questioned Jesus' disciples about Jesus having meals with such people Jesus replied, "I have not come to call respectable people, but outcasts." In other words, **Jesus preached inclusiveness and believed in bringing outcasts into the mainstream of society**.

<u>Adultery: Judging Others</u>

One morning Jesus was teaching in the temple where people had gathered around him. At that time the teachers of the Law and Pharisees brought a woman and said to Jesus, "This woman was caught in the very act of committing adultery." They then continued by stating that the Law says that such a woman must be stoned to death. Hearing this, Jesus bent over and wrote on the ground by his finger, "Whichever one of you has committed no sin may throw the first stone at her." (John 8:7). On hearing this they all left. Then Jesus told the woman to go home and not to sin again. **Jesus not only believed in forgiving the sinner but also warned people about having double standards.**

3.4 JESUS ESTABLISHES AN ORGANIZATION AND CONTINUES PREACHING AND HEALING

Jesus visited many villages and towns and spread the Good News about the Kingdom of God. He taught in synagogues, explained the real meaning of the Laws to the common people, removed their misconception about right and wrong and healed sick people from their diseases. He was in great demand. People from allover the land wanted to hear him and be cured from all kinds of diseases. Jesus realized that he alone can not do all this by himself and he needed to delegate the work to his disciples. According to Matthew (9:37 & 38), Jesus related the need for such delegation to his disciples this way, "The harvest is large, but there are few workers to gather it in. Pray to the owner of the harvest that he will send out workers to gather in his harvest." This was a great way of communicating to his followers that there was a great need for dedicated workers to do God's work. Jesus' teachings implied that the work was to help the sick and the poor and spread the Good News.

Selection of Twelve Apostles and Instructions to Apostles

Jesus called his disciples and chose twelve of them as his special disciples, whom he named apostles; their names were:
1. Simon (whom he named Peter);
2. Andrew (Simon's brother);
3. James;
4. John (brother of James);
5. Philip;
6. Bartholomew;
7. Thomas;
8. Matthew (the tax collector);
9. James;
10. Thaddaeus;
11. Simon (who was called Patriot); and
12. Judas Iscariot who later betrayed Jesus.

Jesus gave them authority to teach people, help them, drive out evil spirits and cure their diseases. These were Jesus' chosen followers and his helpers. This special group of twelve men is called Apostles. Jesus then sent them out with the following instructions (and with a few warnings):

- Go and teach the people of Israel that "The Kingdom of heaven is near!"
- Heal the sick and serve the poor,
- Give without being paid,
- You will be persecuted for what you will do and say. Do not worry. When time comes you will be rewarded.
- "If anyone declares publicly that he belongs to me, I will do the same for him before my Father in heaven."
- Follow in my steps; this instruction implies, "follow what I do, not only what I say."

Jesus Continues Preaching and Teaching

After giving instructions to his twelve disciples, Jesus himself moved on to towns and villages to preach and serve humanity. During his preaching, healing, and serving the poor and the weak, Jesus found out that in a town, where he had done this the most, many people did not turn away from their sins. Jesus scolded them and said that on the judgment day God will not show mercy on them. Jesus emphasized that merely claiming to be his disciples will not help them. He stressed to his audience that **their salvation will only come if they turned away from their sins**. In other words, even his disciples will have no place in heaven if they engaged in sinful acts.

Jesus also questioned the rigidity with which the Laws of Moses were being interpreted and applied. His explanation was that God gave the Laws for well being of the humanity. **Jesus did not believe in the fundamental misinterpretation of the Laws**. This is exhibited by **two instances**. The **first one** is, when on a Sabbath day, Jesus was walking with his disciple through wheat fields. His disciples were hungry. So they began picking heads of wheat and ate the grain. On seeing this, the Pharisees said that this act of picking the grain on the Sabbath was against the Law. Jesus cited an instance when once David and his hungry men went into the house of God and ate the bread which could only be eaten by the priests. Jesus also questioned the Law which allowed the priests to break the Law in the temple on every Sabbath. Jesus then said that kindness towards the fellow men is more important than mere misinterpretation of the Law. He was also saying that you can not have the Law applied to different people in different ways, i.e. there has to be equity in the application of the Law. The **second** instance was when Jesus healed a paralyzed man on the Sabbath. When some people accused Jesus "of doing wrong" since he was healing on Sabbath, Jesus said that a person will rescue his sheep that fell into a deep hole on the Sabbath. He then continued by saying that a man is worth more than a sheep. Therefore the Law does allow us to help someone on the Sabbath. Jesus thus gave a human face and soul to the Laws which were their original intents.

Jesus was a very effective communicator. He knew his audience and the message he was going to deliver. He always used common man's language in his teachings and effectively drove his points by narrating related stories or **parables**. The following presents a few examples of his effective use of this technique.

1. The Parable of the Sowing Seed: Understanding & following the Message

Once when Jesus was teaching at a lakeside, the crowd became very large. He then went up into a boat and sat on it. Jesus then narrated the storey of a man who went out to sow grain. Jesus said that as the man scattered the seed in the field some of it <u>fell on along the path</u>; these seeds were eaten by the birds. Some of the seed fell on the *rocky ground* with very shallow soil depth. Although these seeds soon sprouted but the plants had very shallow roots therefore as soon as the sun came up they dried up. Other seeds fell among thorny bushes. As these bushes grew up they chocked these young plants. Jesus continued by saying that the seeds that fell on good soil grew up as plants that bore grains: "some had one hundred grains, others sixty and others thirty." Jesus then explained the meaning of this parable as follows:

Jesus said that the meaning applies to some of you who hear the message about the **Kingdom of God** but <u>do not understand it.</u> They are like the <u>seed that fell along the path</u>; they lose all they sow. Those who receive the message gladly but the message does not sink deep into them, *give up as soon as trouble or persecution comes* to them because of the message. They are like the seeds that fell on *rocky ground*. There are people who hear the message but because of worries about this life and <u>love for riches choke the message</u>; they are like the <u>seeds that fell among thorn bushes</u>. Finally, those who hear the message about the Kingdom of God understand it and *follow it faithfully*, are like the *seeds that fell on good soil*: "they bear fruits."

2. The Parable of the Weeds

Once a man's servants came to him and reported weeds among his wheat plants. They asked their master, "Sir, it was <u>good seed</u> you sowed in your field: where did these *weeds* come from?" The man answered that it was some enemy's act that he had weeds among his wheat plants. The man instructed his servants not to pull up the weeds now when the wheat plants are small. He said if they pulled them up now then there is a chance of wheat plants getting harmed. The right thing would be to pull up the *weeds at the harvest time*, then tie them and *burn them*. He instructed them that they should then <u>gather the wheat and store them</u> appropriately.

Jesus then explained that the man who sowed the good seed is the Son of Man, the field is the world, the <u>good seeds are the people who belong to the Kingdom of God</u> and the weeds are the *people who belong to the Evil* one sowed by the Devil. The end of the age will be the harvest time when angels will gather all sinners and throw them into "fiery furnace" to burn. The good people will happily live in "their Father's Kingdom."

3. The Parables About the Kingdom of Heaven

Jesus then told his audience numerous parables about The Kingdom of heaven. A few of them are described here. He said that the Kingdom of heaven is like a small mustard seed which when grows up to become the biggest of all plants. "It becomes a tree, so that birds come and make their nests in" it. Jesus also said that the Kingdom of heaven is also like a situation where a man looking for fine pearls finds one. He then "sells everything he has, and buys that pearl." The Kingdom of heaven can also be compared with a scenario in which some fishermen catch all kinds of fish in their net. When they pull it to the shore, they put good ones into the basket but throw away the worthless. The same way at the end of the age, the angels will throw the evil people in the fiery furnace and the good people will go to the Kingdom of heaven.

Spread of the Good News Suppressed: First Violent Action by the Governor but People Still Kept Faith Because of Jesus

John the Baptist was preaching the Good News to the people. He was urging them to turn away from their sins and change their ways. John's message was the same to all irrespective of their position and status in the society. Therefore, John also reprimanded Governor Herod who was engaged in many evil things. In retaliation, Herod put John in the prison. Actually, Herod wanted to kill John but was afraid of the Jewish people who considered John to be a prophet. At the insistence of his wife, Herodias, Herod ordered John to be beheaded. He thus thought that the spread of the Good News to the common masses can be throttled. On hearing the news that **John the Baptist had been beheaded** in the prison, Jesus became sad and left Galilee in a boat and went to a lonely place by himself. When people heard about this, they followed him via land route and greeted him when he got out of the boat. Seeing this, Jesus' heart was filled with emotions "and he healed their sick."

It was already late in the evening and the place was quite lonely and far away from the towns and villages. There were **five thousand men** not counting women and children who came to see and hear Jesus. Jesus' disciples urged him to send the people away so that they could go and feed themselves since they had only five loaves of bread and two fish to eat. Jesus asked the people to sit down, he then took the food they had and gave thanks to God. He then broke the loaves and gave them to his disciples who in turn gave them to the people. "**Everyone ate and had enough.**"

Jesus, then, told his disciples to go to the other side of the lake and he himself went up a hill to pray. Then in the morning Jesus came to his disciple "**walking on the water.**" Seeing this, his disciples got terrified. Jesus advised them to have **courage and faith**. At Peter's request Jesus made it possible for him also to walk with him on water. Seeing this Jesus' disciples exclaimed, "**Truly you are the Son of God.**" Jesus then walked along by the Lake Galilee and climbed a hill and sat down. As large crowds came with their lame, blind and dumb and assembled around him, Jesus cured them all. Thus, Jesus made **the lame walking, the blind seeing and the dumb speaking**. Seeing this people "praised the God of Israel."

Jesus **rebuked the religious leaders** who only cared about strictly following the outwardly religious rituals. Jesus insisted that the things that come out of your mouth make you clean or unclean. Because what comes out of your mouth comes from ones heart. For example, evil ideas coming from your heart may result in killing, adultery and evil things. Therefore, one should worry less about outward cleanliness and more about the cleanliness of the soul and the heart.

Jesus Speaks about Peter's Strong Faith in God and His Own Future Sufferings as He Continues Teaching

Jesus knew that the trust and the faith of his disciples in God and in him was very important in spreading the message about God and turning people away from their sins. He therefore asked his disciples the question about himself, "Who do you say I am." In response to this Peter answered, "You are the Messiah, the son of the living God." Jesus knew about his future sufferings and eventual crucifixion. He then addressed to Peter and said that **Peter was a rock of his faith** and on such a rock foundation, Jesus said, "I will build my church, and not even death will ever be able to overcome it."

Realizing how Pharisees and other leaders of the religion were plotting against him and how his following was increasing in large numbers, Jesus decided to confront the elders and the chief priest in Jerusalem because they were misleading the masses. He knew that if he spoke against the wrong doers especially those with vested interest, they will not let him live. He also realized that John the Baptist was, earlier, beheaded because of his speaking up against them. Jesus then said that he will go to Jerusalem and suffer from, "the teachers of the Law. **I will be put to death, but three days later I will be raised to life**." Jesus also spoke about his future suffering at three different occasions.

Jesus then taught his disciples about being humble and kind to others and also talked about divorce. While talking about divorce he also provided clarification on the definition of adultery. These three teachings were given by Jesus to his disciples in the following manner:

1. *Humble*: Jesus was asked by his disciples, "Who is the greatest in the Kingdom of heaven?" Jesus then called on a child, had him stand in front of him and then replied, "The **greatest** in the Kingdom of heaven **is the one who humbles himself** and becomes like this child. And whoever welcomes in my name one such child as this, welcomes me" (Matthew 18:4 and 5).

2. *Kind to Others*: Once a teacher of the Law began discussions with Jesus about the love for God, and the love for your neighbor. When the issue about, "Love your neighbor as you love yourself" came up for explanation, the teacher asked Jesus about the real meaning of, "Who is your neighbor?" Jesus then answered this by citing the parable of **the Good Samaritan**. He narrated the story by saying that once a man was traveling from Jerusalem to Jericho. On his way, he was robbed, beaten and left on the way half dead. After this crime was committed and the man was left on the wayside to die, it happened that a priest was going that way. The priest saw the man and walked away without doing anything. Similarly, a Levite did

the same. Then a Samaritan saw the injured man. He went to the man, cleaned his wounds, put bandages on his wounds, put him on his animal, took him to an inn and paid money to the innkeeper for the man's care until his wounds are healed. During this discussion it was then concluded that among these three people, the priest, the Levite and the Samaritan, the **Samaritan was kind to the wounded man and acted like a neighbor.**

3. *Divorce and Adultery:* Once Jesus was preaching and healing in the territory of Judea on the other side of the River Jordan. Then some Pharisees asked him to clarify about the Law of divorce. They asked if a man can divorce his wife for whatever reason he wishes. This is an important question because we have heard a typical instance where a woman was being stoned for adultery but did not hear such instances for a man being caught in adultery case. This exhibits an unequal application and interpretation of the Law. Jesus then provided a just and equal clarification of the Law of divorce by saying, " any man who divorces his wife for any cause other than her unfaithfulness, commits adultery if he marries other woman" (Matthew 19:9).

Jesus Reinforces and Defines Commandments

In response to a man's question on how to receive eternal life, Jesus said, "Keep the commandments if you want to enter life." Jesus further explained about these commandments as follows:

- Do not commit murder.
- Do not commit adultery.
- Do not steal.
- Do not accuse anyone falsely.
- Respect your father.
- Respect your mother.

At a later time, in response to a question from some Pharisees, Jesus added that the two most important commandments in the Law were:
- Love the Lord your God with all your heart, with your soul, and with all your mind.

- Love your neighbor as you love yourself.

3.5 JESUS' ENTRY INTO JERUSALEM

As mentioned earlier, after preaching, healing and teaching in the towns and villages and having large crowds following him all over the land, Jesus decided to go to Jerusalem to bring the Good News to the elders and the priests in Jerusalem. As Jesus and his disciples approached Jerusalem, the news of his coming spread fast and large crowds came to greet and join him. The crowd began shouting in praise of God and the prophet Jesus; this is what they called him.

Then Jesus went to the temple and saw the tables of moneychangers and the stools of those who sold pigeons. Seeing this made Jesus unhappy. He, therefore overturned their tables and stools and drove out who were doing buying and selling in the Temple. Jesus also healed the blind and the crippled that came to him to be cured. He also said to all present that the Temple is for prayers, not for "making it a hideout for thieves." The chief priests and the teachers of the Law became angry to see what Jesus was doing. On the other hand, good people whose souls were clean and had turned away from their sins praised Jesus for his good deeds.

Jesus Speaks Against the Establishment

Jesus spoke against the Pharisees and the chief priests who would not turn away from their sins and would still mislead the people because this was in their personal interest. He did not directly attack them but narrated the story of "the tenants in the vineyard." The parable went like this: Once there was a landowner who planted a vineyard. He then rented the vineyard to the tenants and left home for a trip. When he came back he sent his slaves to receive his share of the crop. The tenants beat some of them and killed others. Then he sent his son and the tenants killed him too. Finally, when he went they treated him the same way. Then, Jesus concluded by saying, "*the Kingdom of God will be taken away from you and given to a people who will produce the proper fruits.*" This introduces the concept that the **producer is superior to the bureaucratic absentee landlord**. The Pharisees and the chief priests understood this and realized that Jesus was talking about them. Although they wanted to arrest Jesus but could not do so since crowds considered Jesus to be a prophet. This shows that by this time, a large part of the population agreed with what Jesus was preaching and the establishment was afraid of him because of his large following.

There were many social, religious and political forces active in the land during this time. Pharisees and Sadducees were trying to influence the Jewish population by giving their own narrow interpretation of the Laws of Moses and the Old Testament. On the other hand, there was a political party of influence called Herod's party which was composed of Jews who favored being ruled by one of the descendents of Herod the Great rather than by the Roman Governor (Good News New Testament, 1977). All these groups were trying to influence the Jewish population. So when they realized that Jesus' influence was growing in the population they wanted to discredit him. One way to do this, they thought, was to make Jesus speak against the Roman emperor so that he could be charged with propagating ideas against the ruler and be arrested. So they asked him if he supported or opposed paying taxes to the Emperor. Jesus understood their trick of entrapment. He replied, "Pay to the Emperor what belongs to the Emperor and pay to God what belongs to God." This statement has a great political and religious implication. This can be interpreted as **the concept of separation of the church and the state**.

Practice What You Preach: Jesus Condemns Hypocrisy

Jesus spoke to his disciples and the crowds that came to hear him, about the importance of **humility, justice and honesty**. He said that it was important to be humble. On the other hand, some teachers of Law liked to be called "Teacher" or others liked to be called "Leader" but in reality they were neither a Teacher nor a Leader. They only spoke great words and claimed to know the Law. But they did not follow what they spoke and preached. All these people did was that they showed off their robes and exhibited straps with verses from the scriptures. Their actions were contrary to what they said. Jesus condemned them and warned his disciples against following them. He stressed that the doors to the Kingdom of heaven were permanently closed for such hypocrites. Jesus condemned those who believed that God will be pleased by following religious rituals, such as, offering a percentage of their income in the form of seasoning herbs. He emphasized that the Law tells you to be just, merciful and honest in your daily life. Jesus experienced that the so called leaders and teachers, such as, the priests and Pharisees were not following the Law in their daily lives. They were preaching it to others without practicing what they were teaching; this he said was hypocrisy.

Jesus Talks About the Future of Humanity

Jesus' disciples came to him and asked, "Tell us when all this will be, and what will happen to show that it is the time for your coming and the end of the age." Matthew (24:3), Mark (13:3) and Luke (21:7) also present the similar question that was posed to Jesus by his disciples. Jesus first warned his disciples about false Messiahs who will claim to be the real one. He said that people should not be fooled by such claims. He then said that there will be many battles, many wars, natural calamities, such as, earthquakes and floods. But they do not mean that the end was coming. He also said that there will be many persecutions of his followers and many betrayals among brothers and their faith in him will be tested. Jesus continued by saying that those who hold out to the end will be saved. The end will only come when "this Good News about the Kingdom will be preached through all the world for a witness to all mankind." (Matthew 24:14). Jesus continued by saying that no one (neither the angel nor the Son) really knows that day and hour; only the Father knows about this. This shows that Jesus was honest about what he knew and clearly confessed that it is God who knows everything not him. This was unlike many other Teachers of his time who claimed to know all.

The Righteous People & the Final Judgment

Although, Jesus said, that he did not know the day and hour when the end of the age will come but, he said, when it comes the Son of Man will gather the people of all nations before him. He will then place the righteous people at his right and others at his left. Then he will say to the people on his right "Come and possess the Kingdom" of heaven. According to Matthew (25:

35 & 36), Jesus said that the Son of Man will tell them this is because, "I was hungry and you fed me, thirsty and you gave me a drink; I was stranger and you received me in your homes, naked and you clothed me; I was sick and you took care of me, in prison and you visited me." Jesus further said that, "you did this for one of the least of these brothers of mine, you did it for me!" This teaching of Jesus has had the most important impact and influence on his true followers during and after his death. They have faithfully served and cared the poorest of the poor and weakest of the weak, irrespective of their nationality and faith throughout the centuries. This has motivated numerous individuals to do charity work and some of them even dedicated their entire lives in the service of humanity, especially for those who have been the most unfortunate ones: *what a powerful message.*

3.6 JESUS ARRESTED AND CRUSIFIED

After Jesus finished teaching the gist of all these good messages to his disciples, he told them that the Son of Man will soon be "handed over and crucified." In the meantime the chief priests and the elders, who had vested interest in keeping the status quo, unlike the common Jewish man, made plans to arrest Jesus secretly. They decided not to do this during the Passover Festival because they feared that the people will riot if Jesus was arrested during this time.

<u>Last Supper & Jesus Arrested</u>

Jesus told his disciples to arrange the Passover celebration at a man's house whose name was suggested by Jesus himself. His disciples complied with the suggestion and prepared the Passover meal when they assembled there. Then Jesus sat with his twelve disciples to eat. During the meals he "took a piece of bread, gave a prayer of thanks, broke it, and gave it to his disciples. He then said "take it, this is my body." Then he took a cup, gave thanks to God, and gave it to them. "Drink it, all of you," he said; "this is my blood, which seals God's covenant, my blood poured out for many for the forgiveness of sins" (Matthew 26: 26, 27 & 28). After the meals they all went to the Mount of Olives. The mood in the assembly was very somber. Jesus then went with his disciples to a place called Gethsemane. He was filled with grief. He expressed his feelings by saying' "The sorrow in my heart is so great that it almost crushes me." While Jesus was talking, one of the twelve disciples, named Judas Iscariot arrived. He had betrayed their teacher; he had brought with him armed men hired by the chief priests and the elders to arrest Jesus. According to Matthew (26: 56) "Seeing this all the disciples left him and ran away." Jesus was then arrested by these armed men.

Jesus Presented Before the Council and Then Handed Over to the Roman Governor

After his arrest, Jesus was taken by force to the house of the High Priest. As expected the teachers of the Law and the elders had gathered at this house. As has been mentioned above, these people represented the corrupt establishment and were misrepresenting the Laws. In this process, they were responsible for exploitation of the Jewish masses. Jesus, on the other hand, was preaching to help the common man, speaking against the superstitions and the corrupt establishment supported by the Roman rulers. The masses supported Jesus and considered him the Messiah. Jesus was then presented before the chief priests and the whole council who tried to fabricate false evidence against him but they were unsuccessful. After some cross examination the establishment, based on the misrepresentation of what Jesus has been preaching, falsely charged Jesus with "Blasphemy." Then in the early morning, all the chief priests and the elders put Jesus in chains and handed him to the Roman governor, Pilate.

Crucifixion and Death of Jesus

The Roman governor, Pilate, then questioned Jesus about the correctness of the charges levied against him. He was asked if he agreed or disagreed with the accusations of the elders and the chief priests. He was given a chance to make statement(s) in this regards. Jesus, however, refused to answer. Then the governor had Jesus whipped. Following this, the governor "handed him over to be crucified." The Pilate's soldiers then took Jesus into the governor's palace, mistreated him and made fun of him. After that the soldiers led him out for crucifixion. "He went out, carrying his cross." "There they crucified him; and they also crucified two other men, one on each side, with Jesus between them" (John 19:18). Jesus saw his mother and the disciple, he loved, standing there. He then said to his mother, "He is your son." Also he said to his disciple, "She is your mother." The disciple then took Jesus' mother, Mary, in his home (John 19:26 & 27). In the afternoon, Jesus died on the cross. Then the people gathered around there went home, "beating their breasts in sorrow" (Luke 23: 48).

The Burial and The Resurrection of Jesus

In the evening a rich man named Joseph, who was also Jesus' disciple, arrived there. He obtained the governor's permission for Jesus' body. Joseph had recently dug out a tomb out of solid rock for himself. He took Jesus' body, "wrapped it in a new linen sheet, and placed it in his own tomb." He then "rolled a large stone across the entry of the tomb and went away" (Matthew 27: 59 & 60). On Sunday morning, when Mary Magdalene and Mary (mother of James and Joseph) went to look at the tomb they heard a violent earthquake and an angel of the Lord appeared and said to them, "Jesus has been raised." Then the angel told the women to go to his disciples and tell them that they should go to Galilee where they will see Jesus who has gone there, ahead of them.

Hearing this, the eleven disciples went to the hill in Galilee. On seeing him they worshiped him. According to Matthew (28: 19 & 20) Jesus then said to his disciples, "Go, then, to all peoples everywhere and make them my disciples: baptize them in the name of the Father, the Son, and the Holy Spirit, and teach them to obey everything I have commanded you. And I will be with you always, to the end of the age."

Jesus' dedicated disciples throughout the centuries have been faithfully following this command, some with greater success than others; nonetheless they have tried their best.

3.7 OVERVIEW AND JESUS' GIFT TO HUMANITY

After leading Israelites out of slavery, in Egypt, Moses established an orderly organization consisting of judges, priests, and other officials. He also outlined the requirements for a place of worship, and laid down the rules and regulations for smooth running of a civil and a just society. After conquering the land of Canaan, the Israelites lived and flourished in their promised land for many centuries. With time, the Israelite society achieved cultural, economical, and political maturity. However, as time passed, they were attacked, defeated, exiled and ruled by foreigners. During this period, almost entire middle-east was under Roman Empire. With defeats, exile, and now under foreign rule, the general population became poor and the priests and the local rulers, in general, became self centered and rigid in their interpretation of the Law. The weaker and the poorer Israelites were suffering the most. The people were, therefore, looking for a Messiah who could save them from such a miserable state. This was the time when Jesus was born in Bethlehem to Mary, who was married to Joseph. Jesus was a descendent of King David who was a descendent of Abraham.

Out of the fear for their son's life from Herod, the king of Judea, who had ordered to kill all baby boys in Bethlehem, Joseph and Mary left for Egypt with their infant son. After the death of King Herod, Joseph came back to Israel with his family and settled in the town of Nazareth in Galilee. As time passed, Jesus grew up to be a healthy and wise man. He learned from Jewish teachers and became well versed in the Jewish theology and the Law. During this time, John the Baptist was preaching about the God and was teaching people to turn away from their sins. When people confessed their sins and vowed to lead honest and pure life, John baptized them in the River Jordan. Jesus was greatly impressed by John's teachings and the good work he was doing to keep people away from their sins. He then came to John and requested to be baptized. As soon as he was baptized, Jesus was filled with spirituality "and he saw the Spirit of God coming down like a dove and lighting on him."

Jesus, then, began preaching in synagogues. His main message in all his religious and social reformist teachings was: "**Turn away from your sins, because the Kingdom of heaven is near**!" As Jesus continued his teachings, his fame and good name spread throughout the territory of Galilee and people came to hear him from all over the land. As large crowds followed Jesus to hear him, he went up a hill and began teaching. Some of his key teachings on the hill (known as the Sermon on the Mountain) were as follows:

1. Happiness: Jesus said that true happiness is attained by those who are humble, are merciful to others, work for peace, and are pure in heart.

2. Laws of Moses and Teachings of the Prophets: Jesus emphasized that his teachings do not say that people should do away with these laws and teachings. Jesus said that he was simply explaining them in simple language. He stressed that instead of doing away with the laws people should make sure to follow them.

3. Anger Control: Jesus said that in addition to the commandment of "Do not commit murder" one should also get rid of anger. He said that "whoever calls his brother a worthless fool will be in danger of going to the fire of hell." Jesus continued by saying "make peace with your brother."

4. Adultery: Further explanation and extension of the law that states "Do not commit adultery" is that if anyone casts his eyes "at a woman and wants to possess her is guilty of committing adultery."

5. Revenge: Jesus revised the earlier preaching, by others, stating "an eye for an eye, and a tooth for a tooth" to "Do not take revenge." On the contrary he preached forgiveness and said, "If anyone slaps you on the right cheek, let him slap your left cheek too."

6. Charity: Those who have been blessed with wealth should give something to needy people. However, such charity should not be done publicly. In other words "do not make a big show of it."

7. Prayer: Prayer should be in simple language and should be done in private. Do not make it a big public show "like the hypocrites" do.

8. Judging Others: If you want to be a good person in God's eyes "Do not judge others."

9. Treating Others: Generally people complain about other people's behavior towards them but do not notice their own behavior. Jesus therefore said, "Do for others what you want them to do for you."

10. False Prophets: Jesus warned people against false prophets. He advised people to be on your guard against false prophets because "they come to you looking like sheep on the outside, but on the inside they are really like wild wolves."

11. Obeying and Practicing These Teachings: Jesus said just hearing the words of his teachings and not obeying them is wrong. He said that obeying and practicing these teachings is like building a house on rock that will stay intact under sever winds, rain and floods.

Then, Jesus continued preaching and spreading the Good News about the Kingdom of God in many villages, towns and synagogues. People from all over the land wanted to hear him and be cured from all kinds of diseases. Jesus frequently used **parables** to communicate his ideas to his audience. Although he was a very effective communicator, he realized that he could not do all this work by himself. Therefore, he decided to delegate authority to do all this work to a select group of **twelve of his disciples**; this group of twelve men is also called **Apostles.** Jesus then sent out this select group of disciples with the following instructions:

- Go and teach the people of Israel that "The Kingdom of heaven is near!"
- Heal the sick and serve the poor,
- Give without being paid,
- You will be persecuted for what you will do and say. Do not worry. When time comes you will be rewarded.

- "If anyone declares publicly that he belongs to me, I will do the same for him before my Father in heaven."

- Follow in my steps; this instruction implies, "follow what I do, not only what I say."

After giving these instructions to his disciples, Jesus himself went on to the towns and villages to preach his message and to serve the humanity. This was Jesus' first and the most important decision to prepare his disciples to keep on serving the weak and the poor and continue spreading the Good News about the kingdom of heaven in his absence.

Jesus firmly believed in following the Ten Commandments. He stressed the need to follow them. In his teachings, Jesus said that one must follow the Commandments and defined them as follows:

- **Do not commit murder.**
- **Do not commit adultery.**
- **Do not steal.**
- **Do not accuse anyone falsely.**
- **Respect your father.**
- **Respect your mother**.

At a later time, in response to a question from some Pharisees, Jesus added that the two most important commandments in the Law are:

- **Love the Lord your God with all your heart, with your soul, and with all your mind.**
- **Love your neighbor as you love yourself.**

Jesus went to Jerusalem to bring the Good News to the elders and the priests. He also went to the Temple to heal and spoke strongly against the people who were buying and selling in the Temple. He also pointedly spoke against hypocrisy. He condemned those whose actions were contrary to what they preached. This made the Pharisees and the chief priests very unhappy.

Jesus talked about the end of the age and the righteous people. He said that the Kingdom of heaven will belong to the righteous people because, "**I was hungry and you fed me, thirsty and you gave me a drink; I was stranger and you received me in your homes, naked and you clothed me; I was**

sick and you took care of me, in prison and you visited me." Jesus further said that, **"you did this for one of the least of these brothers of mine, you did it for me!"** This teaching of Jesus has had the most important impact and influence on his true followers during and after his death. They have faithfully served and cared the poorest of the poor and weakest of the weak, irrespective of their nationality and faith throughout the centuries. This has motivated numerous individuals to do charity work and some of them even dedicated their entire lives in the service of humanity, especially for those who have been the most unfortunate ones: *this has proven to be a very powerful message for service to the humanity.*

After Jesus' crucifixion and subsequent resurrection, he met his disciples on the hill in Galilee and said, **"Go, then, to all peoples everywhere and make them my disciples: baptize them in the name of the Father, the Son, and the Holy Spirit, and teach them to obey everything I have commanded you. And I will be with you always, to the end of the age."**

The above messages truly propagate universal brotherhood for all, irrespective of ones religious affiliation, nationality and ethnicity; truly for those who belong to the Kingdom of God. The Kingdom of heaven will belong to all those who turn away from their sins and serve the poor, the sick, the weak, and the downtrodden.

4

MUHAMMAD

4.1 ARABIA PRIOR TO AND AT THE TIME OF MUHAMMAD'S BIRTH

Political, Social and Economical Conditions of Arabia Prior to and at the Time of Muhammad's Birth

As shown in **Figure 4.1,** the Arabian Peninsula, where Muhammad was born, is very large in size. Barring a few small coastal areas, the Arabian land has desert climate with very little rainfall. During the early part of the fifth and sixth century A.D., on the southern part of the peninsula, lied the Kingdom of Yemen, whose people were politically and intellectually cut off from the rest of the Arabian Peninsula. Yemen had been involved in the world politics for a long time. This is because of its natural location suited for caravan route from Syria and Egypt as well as for ships plying between the Indian Ocean and the Red Sea. Because of this reason the South Arabian colonies were established at along the caravan routes. However, it can be said that Islam (which was started in the seventh century A.D.) is primarily the creation of the western and somewhat central Arabia's political, social and economic culture which actually, was culturally quite different from the southern peninsula.

During the sixth century A.D., the political and the economic powers, in the south, were concentrated in the towns and the states. On the contrary, everywhere else in the peninsula, the power was mostly dispersed into nomadic tribes with a few exceptions of a few small urban units. The tribes formed and broke alliances among themselves easily. They were, thus, also autonomous. In the north and the central Arabic world, members of the "great families" felt a bond among themselves because they were bound together in a hierarchical order (Von Grunebaum, 1970). The individuals in this system felt that they were first and foremost a member of his tribe; thus their security and the existence was made possible through the community of the tribe.

It is generally recognized that camel was introduced in Arabia many centuries earlier. This made the camel breading Bedouin Arabs masters of the desert since a camel can carry on an average over 250 kilograms load covering up to approximately 160 kilometers a day and can stay up to eight days without water. In spite of this great mobility, no large empires were established in Arabia. During the fourth and the fifth century A.D., however, there were three buffer states established within the boundaries of the Arabic Peninsula at the initiatives of the Byzantines, the Persians, and the Yemenites. Bedouin still roamed the desert with their "anarchistic leaning". During the centuries prior to the rise of Islam (sixth and the prior centuries), the tribes dissipated their energies in trivial guerilla fighting amongst all.

Sometimes during the late fifth and early sixth century A.D., **the tribe of Quraish** seized **Mecca** and made a sort of working agreement with Kinana Bedouin of the vicinity. Mecca lies in a hot, barren valley and is surrounded

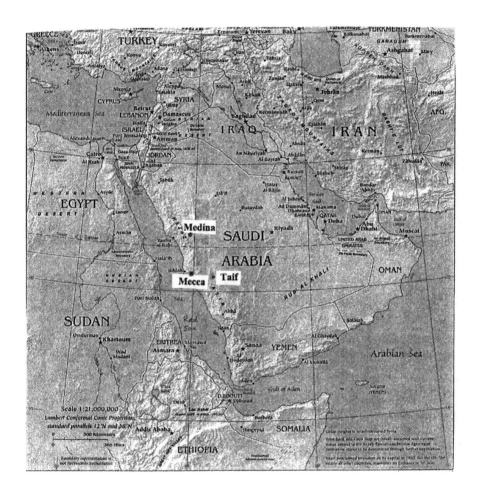

Figure 4.1 Arabian Peninsula Where Muhammad Was Born
(Base Map: Courtesy of The General Libraries UT at Austin, 2003)

by inhospitable mountains. Its economic importance was due to its location on the path of a trade route from modern Iraq to the Red Sea and had a water supply provided by the well, Zemzem. Quraish tribe leaders governed the city while the military protection to the city was the responsibility of Ahabish. Ahabish were of the Abyssinian origin but now also used recruits from minor tribes camping in the neighborhood of Mecca (Von Grunebaum, 1970).

Mecca was mainly sustained by trade and the money spent by the pilgrims. On the other hand Yathrib (later named Medina) and Taif, the two towns, one towards the north and another to the east of Mecca, respectively, were placed in the environment that allowed them some agriculture and thus were better placed by Arab standards of that time. Markets were protected by sacred truce allowing towns to keep hold on long distance trade and Bedouins to exchange goods. Bedouins were still poorer than the town-folks whose contractors controlled the trade. **Polygamy was prevalent and separation was easy.** Life was hard in the desert and this led to hard customs. Although an arbiter (*hakam*) would generally settle disputes, the **mighty appeared to have the rights in most cases.** Across the peninsula, since the fifth and the sixth century A.D., there were political and religious influences at various times by Jews, Christians, and Persians. For example, Christianity was introduced in the South Arabia during the sixth century A.D. During the fourth and fifth century A.D., Judaism had spread in South Arabia after the destruction of temple in Jerusalem. During the late sixth and the early seventh century, Persian rule converted the Yemenite Christians to Nestorianism.

Thus, Christianity and Judaism were adopted by a number of different tribes in Arabia. At the same time, paganism also was practiced by a large number of Arab population. In Mecca, Kaba was the first and the foremost holy places for Arab tribes; each would worship there based on their faith. Most, however, would call, Kaba, the holy place of al-ilah, Allah, "The God". Here, the sanctuary was erected in black stone Kaba (cube) of Mecca. During this period, everywhere in Arabia as well as in Kaba, circumambulation (*tawaf*), standing in worship and bloodless and bloody sacrifices were essential elements of cult practices.

Birth of Muhammad

Muhammad was born into one of the noble families of Mecca in the year 570 A.D. (53 years before the Hijrah, the Islamic calendar). His father's name was Abdullah, son of Abdul Mttalib of the tribe of Quraish and the clan of Hashim. His father died before Muhammad was born and was orphaned early. He was first raised and protected by his grandfather, Abdul Muttalib and after his grandfather's death by his uncle, Abu Talib. Although he lived in close contact with wealth and power, he was poor until his marriage. Traditions relate that before and at Muhammad's birth there were signs and wonders. Not much, however, is either recorded or known about his early adult life.

Thus from Abraham to Muhammad the chronology was as follows:

- **Abraham** had two sons: **Ishmael** and Isaac
- Meccans descended from Ishmael
- **Abdul Muttalib** was a Meccan of the tribe of Quraish and the clan of Hashim
- **Muhammad** was the grandson of **Abdul Muttalib** and son of **Abdullah**

4.2 MUHAMMAD'S LIFE AND EXPERIENCES IN MECCA BEFORE LEAVING FOR YATHRIB (MEDINA)

Muhammad's Early Life and Marriage

As Muhammad was being raised by his uncle, Abu Talib, during the later period of his boyhood, he traveled with him, in Merchants' caravan to Syria. Syria, at that time, was under Christian influence and this must have provided him the exposure to Christian theology. With the travel and trading experiences, Muhammad later on, was hired by a wealthy widow named Khadijah. He then made similar journeys to Syria in the services of Khadijah. Through Khadijah's trusted old servant, who also accompanied Muhammad, she received excellent report on his behavior and his faithful conduct of her business. Soon afterwards, she married her young agent who was fifteen years younger to her. Tradition says that she was forty years old at the time; this would mean that Muhammad was twenty five years old at the time of their marriage. This marriage came about on her initiative and they had twenty six years of their married life together. This marriage gave him freedom of movement and time to think and develop his thoughts. This also gave him rank amongst the notables of Mecca.

Married and having acquired wealth and social recognition, Muhammad now could spend time in his theological pursuit. This he did by associating with the seekers of truth in Mecca and also spending every year, a long period of time, in solitude on the Mountain of Hira, on whose foot Mecca lies.

Muhammad Receives His Call: First Revelation

According to Mohammad Pickthall's (2000) English translation of "the Glorious Qur'an", Meccans claimed their descent from Ishmael, the elder son of Abraham. Tradition stated that their temple at Ka'bah (Kaba) was built by Abraham for the worship of Allah, One God. Although called the house of Allah, the chief object of worship, in this house of Allah were a number of idols which were called "Daughters of Allah". There were a few people in Mecca, who called themselves seekers of truth, who did not agree with this idol worship. This practice of idolatry existed there for centuries and these seekers of truth wanted to find out about the real teachings of Abraham's religion of One God. These seekers of truth, also called *Hunafa*, did not form a community but "each was seeking truth by the light of his own inner consciousness". Muhammad became one of these *Hunafas*.

Every year during the month of Ramadan, Muhammad would go with his family to the Mountain Hira. Here he would go for meditation in a cave. It was here, **when he was forty years old, towards the end of this quiet month of Ramadan, he had his first revelation.** The tradition has it that when he was asleep he heard a heavenly voice commanding Muhammad to "Read". Muhammad replied, "I can not read". This dialogue was repeated the second time. The third time, the voice again commanded Muhammad to read the verse as recorded in the Surah 96: The Clot, of the Qur'an, and is presented below:

"1.Read: In the name of thy Lord who createth, 2.Createth man from a clot, 3. Read: And Thy Lord is the Most Bounteous, 4. Who teacheth by the pen, 5. Teacheth man that which he knew not. 6. Nay, verily man is rebellious, 7. That he thinketh himself independent! 8. Lo! Unto thy lord is the return. 9. Hast thou seen him who dissuadeth, 10. A slave when he prayeth? 11. Hast thou seen if he (relieth) on the guidance (of Allah), 12. Or enjoineth piety? 13. Hast thou seen if he denieth (Allah's guidance) and is forwarded? 14. Is he then unaware that Allah seeth? 15. Nay, but if he cease not. We will seize him by the forelock- 16. The lying, sinful forelock- 17. Then let him call upon his henchmen, 18. We will call the guards of hell. 19. Nay! Obey not thou him. But prostrate thyself, and draw near (unto Allah)."

When Muhammad woke up, he went out of the cave on to the hillside. He again heard the voice that said, "**O! Muhammad you are Allah's messenger, and I am Gabriel**". Then Muhammad saw the angel "in the likeness of a man". When he returned to his wife in distress, she assured him that he was a man of good conduct and hoped that one day he would become the prophet of his people. Although Muhammad was illiterate, the angel on Mt. Hira insisted on his "Reading". Therefore, the sacred book is known as Al-Qua'an- the Reading of the man who knew not how to Read (Pickthall, 2000).

Another revelation that Muhammad received, during this early Meccan revelations, recorded in Surah 112: The Unity, was, as cited below:

"1.Say: He is Allah, the One! 2. Allah, the eternally Besought of all! 3. He begetteth not nor was begotten; 4. And there is none comparable unto Him."

Muhammad's first convert was his wife Khadijah, his second convert was his cousin Ali and the third convert was his servant Zeyd. Among others, of his early converts were his old friend Abu Baker and some of his slaves and dependents. During first three years of his mission, Muhammad only preached to his family and to his intimate friends; the people of Mecca generally regarded him one who had become a little mad. Another revelation, as recorded in Surah 1: The Opening, during this period, which can be said as the essence of Qur'an, is as follows:

"1. Praise to Allah, Lord of the Worlds; 2. The Beneficent and Merciful; 3. Owner of the day of Judgment; 4. Thee (alone) we worship; Thee alone we ask for help; 5. Show us the straight path; 6. The path of those whom Thou hast favored; 7. Not (the path) of those who earn Thine anger nor those who go astray."

These three are the key revelations regarding God, the way they were revealed to Muhammad and have become important to the faithful.

Preaching in Public to All Meccans

Then, at the end of the third year , Muhammad decided to present himself to the Meccans, in public, as the Prophet : the messenger of God. **He now preached openly against idolatry and the folly of worshiping many gods.** This angered Quraish who now became hostile to Muhammad's disciples; especially they began persecuting them. They even wanted to kill Muhammad but the blood- vengeance of Hashim clan, to which he belonged, prevented them from such action. His beliefs were so strong that he continued warning and threatening idolatrous about the consequences of "hell" and "burning in fire". In response, Quraish actively ridiculed his teachings and persecuted his poor followers. In view of this, Muhammad felt compelled to advise his humble followers to migrate to Abyssinia, a Christian country. During this period, he had other revelations which are presented in Surahas 19: Mary; 20 : Ta Ha; 34 : Saba; 35 : The Angel; and others. In these, he mentions the Prophets Abraham and Jesus and recognizes Mary the mother of Jesus as mentioned in the Scriptures. His thrust was that Christians are the people of the book and are believers of One God. By recognizing Abraham, Isaac, Jacob, Moses, Ishmael and Jesus as prophets he was establishing a kinship with Jews and Christians. At the same time, he was warning "Now there hath succeeded them a later generation who have ruined worship and have followed lusts. But they will meet deception" (Surah 19:59; Mary). Thus, in around 615 A.D., Muhammad sent his poor followers to Christian Abyssinia, across the Red Sea, thus protecting them from direct molestation and persecution.

In spite of the emigration and thus reduction in numbers of Muslims in Mecca, the conflict between Muhammad and Quraish in Mecca, was not mitigated. The Prophet was propagating a system of ideas that drew strength from an experience of God. His message was echoing all the standard religious themes which for centuries gone by had been around the Near East. The message, however, was altered and simplified (Von Grunebaum, 1970). In a way, he had the following ideas that were different from the prevailing thinking in Mecca at that time.

- He was presenting One God against the multiplicity of pagan pantheon,
- He was presenting One God against the Trinitarian experience of the Christians, and
- He was presenting the human messenger of the Lord against the divine intermediaries clothed in human form.

Muhammad, in his preaching, continued attacking those who did not agree with him. He and his followers, who belonged, by birth to Meccan society, were safe because they were protected by his kin. Even though now Quraish boycotted Hashimites, many of whom still did not agree with Muhammad's teachings, they still protected him. Towards the end of the year 619 A.D., both his uncle, Abu Talib, head of the clan, and his wife Khadija, his greatest supporter, died. Abu Talib's brother and his successor soon withdrew his protection, allegedly because Muhammad had insisted that since Abu Talib had died as a pagan, he now was in hell (Von Grunebaum, 1970).

The relationship between the idolaters and Muhammad became very bitter as he continued his preaching and it became even worse when Omer, one of their stalwarts, accepted the faith.

During this period, Muhammad had some important revelations that would have many **social impacts**. A few examples are: "**And come not near unto adultery**"; "**slay not your children**, fearing a fall to poverty" – a clear reference to burying alive a female child which was the practice among many Arabs; and "**come not near the wealth of orphan ---**" Surah 17:32, 31, and 34: The Children of Israel).

There are numerous revelations about the **rewards for believers and severe punishment for disbelievers**. For example, according to Surah 18:106 and 107; The Cave: Their punishment is "hell, because they disbelieved ---"; and "those who believe and do good works, there are the Gardens of Paradise for welcome". These were very simple but very powerful messages. He also preached that he had been commanded by God "to be of those who **surrender (unto Him)**", "And to recite the Qur'an ----- **I am only a warner**" (Surah 27: 91 and 92; The Ant). In personal behavior the Prophet also preached, "Be modest in thy bearing and subdue thy voice ----" (Surah 31:19; Luqman). He also stressed that earlier scripture of Moses is presented in Arabic as Qur'an when in Surah 46:12; The Wind Curved Hill, says, "When before it there was the Scripture of Moses, an example and a mercy; and this is a confirming scripture in the Arabic language, that it may warn those who do wrong and bring tidings for the righteous."

All this provided Muhammad a following of the people who received simple but convincingly powerful messages of good deeds. He also convinced Jewish people that he was simply propagating their Scripture's message in Arabic language. On the other hand, he was sending the message to idol worshipers that those who disagreed with him were disbelievers and will be punished in the hell. Thus as the number of his followers increased, his opponents also became more bitter and determined. As opposition to Muhammad's teachings grew rigid, he, now, was having little success in converting the remaining population by preaching. He also made an attempt to preach to the inhabitants of Taif, a city east of Mecca, but was unsuccessful.

Invitation from Yathrib (Medina)

Unlike Mecca which was a homogeneous town, Yathrib, an oasis, was divided into village-like settlements; some of these settlements were fortified with towers. The city had a fertile area of about 60 square kilometers surrounded by steppe and desert. It was dominated by Aus and Khazraj clans who had been in continuous guerilla warfare against each other for generations. The rest of the inhabitants, including three Jewish tribes, were drawn into conflict. However, since the year 617 A.D., after the bloody "Battle of Buath", there was relative peace, interrupted only by occasional acts of vengeance (Von Grunebaum, 1970).

In the year 620 A.D., at the season of the yearly pilgrimage to Mecca, Muhammad met a group of men who heard him gladly. These men had come from Yathrib where learned Jewish rabbis had spoken to the pagans that an Arab Prophet will soon come. They told them that when he comes, the Jews will destroy the pagans. When these men met Muhammad, they recognized him as a prophet as the Jewish rabbis had told them. On their return to Yathrib, they relayed the information to their people; they told them all what they had seen and heard in Mecca. As a result, at the next season of pilgrimage, a deputation from Yathrib, came to meet the Prophet and on meeting him they swore allegiance to him. Then they returned to Yathrib with a Muslim teacher.

In the following year (622 A.D.), seventy three Muslims from Yathrib came to Mecca to invite the Prophet to their city. This city was later named Al-Medinah, "the City" par excellence. It was then that the Hijrah, the flight to Yathrib was decided (Pickthall, 2000).

During this late Meccan period, prior to Hijrah, The Prophet had many revelations concerning God, his role, duty of the faithful and banning social ills. Some of which are, as follows:

In Surah 7:158; The Heights; it is revealed that "-----. **I am the messenger of Allah to you all---. There is no God save Him**.------." For food, certain things were forbidden as revealed in Surah 16:115; the Bee; that "He has forbidden for you carrion and blood and swine-flesh------". Also, according to Surah 22:26, 27 and 29; The Pilgrimage (to Mecca) was revealed by saying, "and (remember) when We prepared for Abraham the place of the (holy) House--------. And proclaim unto mankind the Pilgrimage. They will come unto thee on foot and on every lean camel; they will come from every deep ravine. And let them make an end of their unkemptness and pay their vows and go around the ancient House". Ever since, **Pilgrimage (Al-Haj) to Mecca** has been a very important religious duty of the faithful.

Rewards for being righteous and believer is heaven, gardens enclose and vineyards, and maidens for companions and a full cup (Surah 78; The Tiding). Surah 22:19; The Pilgrimage, also says, "These twain (the believers and the disbelievers) are two opponents who contend concerning their Lord. But for those who disbelieve, garments of fire will be cut out of them; boiling fluid will be poured down on their heads." A pagan Arab practice of burying alive girl-children made the Prophet deeply pained; this he expressed, with deep emotions, in Surah 81; The Overthrowing, which says, "When the sun is overthrown; and when the stars fall; and when the hills are moved; and when the camels big with young are abandoned; and when the wild beasts are herded together; and when the seas rise; and when souls are reunited; and when the girl child that was buried alive is asked; for what sin she was slain;-----." This practice was later banned.

4.3 MUHAMMAD DECIDED TO LEAVE MECCA, SETTLED IN MEDINA AND BEGAN BATTLES WITH MECCANS

Muhammad Leaves Mecca and Reaches Medina

After about two years (between 620 A.D. and 622 A.D.) of negotiations with the representatives from Yathrib (Medina), Muhammad decided on Hijrah (migration to Medina). During this period, the Arab clans Aus and Khazraj of Medina had accepted Islam and the Jewish leaders had decided to help Muhammad. Consequently, it was decided to send, ahead of Muhammad's arrival in medina, some seventy members of his community to Medina. These members left Mecca in the summer of 622 A.D. to form a kind of body guard of *muhajirum* (emigrants) to protect Muhammad when he arrived in the oasis in the September of that year (Von Grunebaum, 1970).

With the decision on Hijrah made, the Muslims began selling their properties in Mecca and then leave for Medina. Abu Baker, Ali and the Prophet himself were last to leave Mecca. When Quraish got the information on this, they decided to kill Muhammad prior to his escape. In view of this, Muhammad left his house in dark. Then he and Abu Bakr went together to a cavern in the desert hills and hid there. During their hiding period, Abu Bakr's son, daughter and herdsmen were bringing food for them after nightfall. When it appeared that Quraish were not looking for them any more, one night Abu Bakr appointed guide brought riding camels and they set out on their long ride to Medina. After traveling for many days, they reached Medina. On seeing them, the people of Medina were delighted. Such was the flight of Muhammad from Mecca to Medina- the Hijrah, which counts the beginning of the Muslim era (Pickthall, 2000). It is believed that this date corresponds to July 16, 622 A.D.

On reaching Medina, Muhammad left the choice of his dwelling place to a form of local practice, which was: where his she-camel stopped he bought the place from its owners and erected a place for prayer. Besides this, he also built huts for his two wives (up to that time), one of whom Aisha, then only nine years old, the daughter of Abu Bakr. With his arrival and settling down in Medina, his previous thirteen years of humiliation, of persecution and of apparent failure were over. This also was the beginning of his ten future years of successes of his mission. Till then, he was a preacher but thereafter he became a ruler of a small state, at first, which in ten years grew to be the empire of Arabia (Pickthall, 2000).

Treaties, Organizations and Battles

As discussed earlier, the population of Medina was divided into various factions. To accomplish his goals, Muhammad needed the unified cooperation of the Meccan emigrants (muhajirums) and the Medinan "helpers" (*ansars*). Also to achieve his goal, in the first year of his reign at Medina, the Prophet also made treaty with the Jewish tribes by giving them civil rights and religious liberty. Having achieved social peace and cooperation from various factions in Medina, the Prophet now diverted his attention in obtaining more resources and achieving financial independence to execute his plans. He decided to accomplish this goal by raiding Meccan caravans. In the second year of the Hijrah, as usual, the Meccan merchant caravan was returning from Syria and was to pass through the general area, close to Medina. The Prophet decided to capture the caravan. Among some of his followers, there was some concern about performing such an act during one of the sacred months. This was then made possible through the revelation as per Surah 2:217; The Cow, which says, "They question thee (O Muhammad) with regard to warfare in the sacred month. Say: warfare therein is a great (transgression), but to turn (men) from the way of Allah, and to disbelieve in Him---- and to expel his people thence, is a greater with Allah; for persecution is worse than killing-------."

As the merchant caravan leader heard of the Prophet's plan to capture the caravan, he sent a camel-rider to Mecca for help. A force of about one thousand men was then sent to Medina to protect the caravan. The fighting ensued, called the **"battle of Badr"**, named after a little market village to the south-west of Medina. The battle was fought around mid-March 624 A.D. (**2 after Hijarah,A.H.**). Although Muslim invaders' numerical strength was about three hundred only, they had an excellent battle strategy, his men were disciplined and they fought with fervor for their cause of

Islam. This resulted in an impressive victory for the Prophet. With this victory, the prophet was able to convince the Muslims that they were being supported by the troops of the angels. This victory enhanced the Prophet's image among his followers and they were also convinced that God was on their side as is evident from Surah 8:17; Spoils of war, which says, "Ye (Muslims) slew them not, but Allah slew them. ------." Having gained a new prestige and enthusiasm, he now diverted his attention to strengthen his power inside. This he did by expelling the first of the three Jewish tribes, in about a month after the battle of Badr. Their weapons and immobile property was taken over by Meccan emigrants. This move also weakened the cause of the undecided Arabs (Hypocrites- as branded in Qur'an) who latter accepted Islam and were absorbed into the Muslim community. At this juncture, in the mind of Muhammad, Jews were even more dangerous than conservative Arabs because they refused to be converted. Their resistance to religious and hence political assimilation denied Muhammad the role of the Prophet. This meant that Jews were now unacceptable to Muslims.

In any case, the victory at Badr gave the Prophet new prestige among Arab tribes. He also received further revelations during this period. According to Surah 2:144; The Cow: the revelation commands to change *Qiblah* (the place to turn their face in prayer) from Jerusalem to Kabah at Mecca. According to another revelation of the same Surah 2:173; it was revealed that, "He hath forbidden you only carrion, and blood and swine-flesh,---." Then, according to Surah 2:185. it was revealed that, "The month of Ramadan in which was revealed the Qur'an,---, let him fast the month,--." Then Surah 2:196, says, "Perform the pilgrimage and visit (to Mecca) for Allah.--." Further, Surah 2:219 reveals that, "They question thee about strong drinks and games of chance, say: in both is great sin,--." Thus Muslims were commanded to:

- Turn their face towards Kabah (at Mecca) in prayer,
- Perform pilgrimage to Mecca,
- Fast during the month of Ramadan,
- Do not eat carrion, blood and swine-flesh, and
- Strong drinks and games of chance are forbidden.

Now with the defeat at Badr, the Meccans had lost their prestige. In order to effectively carry out their foreign trade they needed to regain their lost prestige. Therefore, in the following year, (625 A.D.; 3 A.H.), Meccans mobilized a force of three thousand men and reached Uhud, which is located at the north-west border of Medina. The Prophet's first idea, which was also strongly approved by the "Hyprocrites" or the lukewarm Muslim leaders, was to defend the city. But the Muslims believed that God would help them as He did at Badr and urged that they should put a fight. Finally, the Prophet approved this and Muslims took up positions at Uhud. During this battle, the Prophet received wounds. Following this, gathering around the Prophet, the Muslims retreated, leaving many dead. On the other hand, the Meccans were also exhausted in this battle. They felt that by wounding Muhammad they had taught a lesson to Muslims and it was of no use to fight anymore. Whatever the reason, Meccans left Medina without further aggression. Actually, as can be seen by future events, Meccans' apparent success and withdrawl was a political mistake for them. The battle resulted in a status quo and provided opportunity to the Prophet to reorganize and punish those he felt did not cooperate with him. For example, first, Muhammad provided the theological explanation to the defeat by first "pointing out how God considered that any intervention in their favor would have involved the faithful in yet deeper disgrace", at the same time he also laid responsibility for the misfortune on a section of the troops and said that they were not obedient. His position was further strengthened when he forced the second Jewish tribe, the Banu Nadir, to emigrate and "winning the neutrals by intimidation". Through revelations in various sections of Surah 3; The Family of Imran, the Prophet provided moral support and encouragement to his supporters and blamed "Hypocrites" for their disbelief and for not fighting for his cause (Surah 3:123, 139, 151, and 167). Meccans on the other side, realizing their mistake, were now preparing for a final campaign with a goal to completely destroy the Muslim community.

In the battle of Uhud, many Muslims were killed. Since, in the pagan Arab world women had few rights, the concern for orphans and widows led to a declaration of some rights for women which they were deprived of earlier. These rights were revealed in Surah 4: Women. Some of these were slightly revised later on. Although there are some scholars who place the timing for revelation of Surah 4 between the end of third and the end of fifth year A.H., but it appears more reasonable to place the revelation of Surah 4 during the fourth year of Hijrah (Pickthall, 2000). As mentioned earlier, this Surah provides revelations for women and orphan rights. A few of those rights are mentioned here. For example, Surah 4:2 says, "Give unto orphans their wealth--" ; a man can marry up to four women but "—and if ye fear that ye cannot do justice (to so many) then one (only)----." (Surah 4:3); "And all married women (are forbidden unto you) save those (captives) whom your hand possess –" (Surah 4:24). According to Pickthall (2000), polygamy is the nature of some men in all countries. The Prophet was setting a great example of polygamic marriage for the men of temptation, so that by following this they could live righteous life. The Prophet was allowed to have more wives because he was the head of the state and also he was protecting and supporting women, after the war, who had no where to go. Therefore, with the exception of Ayeshah, all his wives had been widows. This thus set up the rights of orphans and widows of war. Pickthall also suggests that "Al-Islam" did not institute polygamy. It restricted an existing institution by limiting the number of a man's legal wives. In author's opinion, this was applicable to the sixth and seventh century society. According to God's commandments, however, Qur'an reveals one woman for one man. For example, Surah 11:40, says, "when our commandments came to pass ----, We said: Load therin two of every kind, a pair (the male and female),----." Also, Surah 13:3, says, "---and of all fruits he placed therein two spouses (male and female).--." Thus for the sixth and seventh century in Arabian Peninsula where women had almost no rights, Islam provided a legal frame work for their rights. Islam also left doors open for their increased rights on a basic theological basis, i.e. one male and one female spouse.

Meccans Advanced on Medina with Ten Thousand Men But Were Forced to Retreat

Thus, on the one hand, Muhammad was reforming the Arab society and politically unifying them, on the other hand, he was preparing them for defense against any future Meccan attack. Meccans took two years to prepare for another assault on Medina. So in the year 627 A.D. (5 A.H.), with a force of about ten thousand men, they advanced on Medina. The prophet mobilized a force of three thousand against Meccans. Meccans' numerical advantage was not as important as the strength of their cavalry. Their force was composed of Meccans and various other tribes. Therefore, they were not as cohesive and motivated as Muhammad's smaller but unified and well organized army. To contain Meccan's cavalry advantage, Muhammad took the advice of a Persian slave convert, Salman, and dug a ditch (*Khandaq*). This technique was new to Arabs and thus brought the cavalry to a virtual stand still; thus it is called the "**Battle of the Ditch.**" It is also recorded by the historians that Muhammad was also able "to create a breach in the enemy front by diplomatic means." Also, the expelled Jewish tribe of Banu Nadir remained neutral. Furthermore, as time passed in the waiting, a bitter wind blew from the sea which prohibited Meccans to cook food for that period. In addition, it became very difficult for them to maintain the integrity of their tents. Thus, after a two-week period of helplessness and apathy, Meccan forces retired with minimal casualty to Medinite forces. As the threat from Meccans did not exist anymore, Muhammad turned his attention inward. He punished the third and the last Jewish tribe of Medina, Bani Qureyzah, for not cooperating in the battle and executed their men (about six hundred in number) and their women and children were sold in slavery. Medina was now a homogeneous Muslim city, i.e. a cohesive religious community (*umma*).

4.4 MUSLIM UMMA IN MEDIA AND ISLAMIC EXPANSION

After the "Battle of the Ditch", following the expulsion of all the three Jewish tribes from Medina and the acceptance of Islam by all Arab tribes, Medina now became a sovereign and homogeneous Islamic religious community. All the members of this community now accepted "adherence to God and his Prophet" and thus formed a Muslim community called *umma*.

In order to maintain this cohesion between various tribes, who had accepted Islam, Muhammad needed to instill a purpose in their mind; this he realized by continuous expansion of the community. His foremost goal was to conquer Mecca. For this, he needed to weaken their economy. Therefore, during the first month of the year 628 A.D. (6 A.H.), which was inspired by a dream (vision), Muhammad took a "little pilgrimage" to Mecca. This pilgrimage (*Umra*) was taken with fifteen hundred volunteers, most of them were Bedouin. Most of the pilgrims were lightly armed and had taken with them sacrificial beasts. The Meccans became suspicious of their intentions and tried to stop Muhammad on his way. He, however, made to the boundary of haram at Al-Hudaibiya through another route and then initiated negotiations with Meccans. The key elements of the negotiated settlement were that:

- Muslims abandoned their pilgrimage that year and there was to be no hostility for ten years,
- Muslims were promised by Meccans to admit them for pilgrimage for three days in the following year (629 A.D.; 7 A.H.),
- During those three days Meccans were to clear the town , and
- Muhammad guaranteed freedom of alliance for Bedouin and return any Meccan converts to Mecca who came with him to Medina.

The pilgrimage was declared to be complete. They, then, slaughtered the sacrificial beasts and returned back to Medina.

Although the faithful were disappointed, the Prophet remained firm. Surah 48:Victory (Al-Fath), was revealed for this truce. It starts with "In the name of Allah, the Beneficent, the Merciful. Lo! We have given thee (O

Muhammad) a signal victory" (Surah 48:1). The treaty turned out to be very good for the Muslims because it (1) recognized the political existence of the *umma*; (2) put the *umma* as a partner equal to Meccans; (3) provided freedom of association for the Bedouin; and (4) increased numbers of tribes wishing to have association with Medina because they realized their strength and their receiving equal treatment if they became Muslim. Many Meccans also realized this and many of them deserted Mecca and opted to go to the Prophet's side. They were received with open arms because Muhammad needed their administrative experience if he had to successfully manage the affairs of an ever increasing *umma*.

As per agreement, the "little pilgrimage" was performed in 7 A.H. (629 A.D.). In the meantime, Muhammad had secured way to the north by conquering the oasis of Khaibar and allowing its owners, who were Jewish, to stay there but pay a large part of their produce to Muslims. Influential Meccans now began coming to Muslim's side because they now knew that Muslims with their unified community were strong and will be the rulers of the future Arabia. Now, the Prophet visited the holy place in Mecca unopposed. Muslims worshiped there for three days and then in accordance with the terms of the truce withdrew from the holy place.

4.5 PROPHET CONQUERS MECCA

Mecca Occupied

By the end of the year 7 A.H. (629 A.D.), a large population of Mecca had either accepted Islam or became resigned to Muslim's power. In the following year 8 A.H.(630 A.D.), the Prophet organized a large force of all Muslims who were capable of bearing arms. After organizing this force, Prophet Muhammad marched to Mecca. The forces of Quraish, by now completely demoralized, put up token resistance to Muslim's attack. Therefore, the Prophet entered Mecca with his men almost without any resistance as a conqueror. Barring a few exceptions, a general amnesty was announced. The entire population of Mecca, then swore their allegiance to Islam. All idols and idolaters' places of worship were then destroyed at the order of the Prophet.

The loss of power by Quraish in Mecca gave an opportunity to the neighboring tribes (living around Mecca), to seek control of the trade routes for the nomads. Therefore, the tribes of the Thaquif and the Hawazin under the leadership of chief Malik the Hawazin organized a large army to attack Mecca. In response, the Prophet led an army of about twelve thousand men against them. The battle was fought at Huneyn and the enemy was defeated. After this, Muslims seized the town of Taif where the fugitive Hawazin leader had fled. A few months later, the town voluntarily surrendered. The booty of this success was large, which was then distributed to the new Meccan converts.

After the complete victory of Mecca and the neighborhood, the Prophet returned to Al-Medinah.

Prophet Muhammad's Last years: formulation of Religious Laws

Although Mecca was conquered in 8 A.H. (630 A.D.), the official procedure of pilgrimage and the worship at Mecca had not changed. Muslims were performing the worship in their way while pagan Arabs were worshiping in their own manner. Then in the year 9 A.H. (631 A.D.), the Prophet had another revelation as recorded in Surah 9. That year the Prophet sent a message to the leader of the pilgrimage, Abu Bakr, which said that, "after that year Muslims only were to make pilgrimage,----." That proclamation actually ended idol-worship in Arabia. The Surah 9:18; Repentance says, "He only shall tend Allah's sanctuaries who believeth in Allah----".

In the year 10 A.H. (632 A.D.), the Prophet went to Mecca as a pilgrim the last time. During this pilgrimage the last revelation recorded in Surah 110; Succour was revealed which read "1.when Allah's succour and the triumph cometh, 2. And thou seest mankind entering the religion of Allah in troops, 3. Them hymn the praises of thy Lord, and seek forgiveness of him. Lo! He is ever ready to show mercy". This expresses the emotional and ideological fulfillment of Muhammad's mission inside Arabia.

Soon after his return from the pilgrimage, in the year 10 A.H. (632 A.D.), the prophet fell sick and after a short illness, he died on June 6, 632 A.D., 10 A.H. The news of the Prophet's death was communicated to the faithful by Abu Bakr in this manner, "O people! Lo! As for him who used to worship Muhammad, Muhammad is dead. But, as for him who used to worship Allah, Allah is Alive and dieth not" (Pickthall, 2000). This was a very powerful message to the believers.

The Muslim religious practices began taking shape during the Prophet's last years. A few of the main ones as summarized by Von Grunebaum,1970, are as follows:
- Limited polygamy,
- Regulation on inheritance,
- Prohibition on pagan customs, such as wine drinking and eating pork,
- Practice of circumcision,
- New calendar and prohibition of the movable month lunar and solar calendar year,
- The *salat* consisting of a strict sequence of gestures to be performed five times in the day, where possible, in common and under a prayer leader (*imam*),

- Required fasts from the sun rise to sunset for an entire month (of Ramadan), and
- The duty to undertake the *hajj* (pilgrimage to Mecca) at least once in a life time.

Thus, the Prophet, the warner and the messenger, preached the existence of one and the only one God through a series of revelations. He also established a religious-political community of Islam based on equality among its followers.

4.6 OVERVIEW AND MUHAMMAD'S GIFT TO HUMANITY

Arabian Peninsula where Muhammad was born is very large in size. However, it can be said that Islam is primarily the creation of the western and somewhat central Arabia's political, social and economic environment. During the sixth century A.D., the political and the economic powers, in the south, were concentrated in the towns and the states. On the contrary, everywhere else in the peninsula, the power was mostly dispersed into nomadic tribes with a few exceptions of a few small urban units.

Sometimes during the late fifth and early sixth century A.D., **the tribe of Quraish** seized **Mecca** and made a sort of working agreement with Kinana Bedouin of the vicinity. Mecca lies in a hot, barren valley and is surrounded by inhospitable mountains. Its economic importance was due to its location on the path of a trade route from modern Iraq to the Red Sea and had a water supply provided by the well, Zemzem. Quraish tribe leaders governed the city while the military protection to the city was the responsibility of Ahabish.

Mecca was mainly sustained by trade and the money spent by the pilgrims. On other hand Yathrib (later named Medina) and Taif, the two towns, one north and another to the east of Mecca, respectively, were placed in the environment that allowed them some agriculture and thus were better placed by Arab standards of that time. **Polygamy was prevalent and separation was easy.** Life was hard in the desert and this led to hard customs. Although arbiter (*hakam*) would generally settle disputes, **might seemed to be the right in most cases.** Across the peninsula, since the fifth and the sixth century A.D., there were political and religious influences at various times by Jews, Christians, and Persians. Thus, Christianity and Judaism were adopted by a number of different tribes in Arabia. At the same time, paganism also was practiced by a large number of Arab population. In Mecca, Kaba was the first and the foremost holy places for Arab tribes; each would worship there based on their faith. Most, however, would call, Kaba, the holy place of al-ilah, Allah, "The God". Here, the sanctuary was erected in black stone Kaba (cube) of Mecca.

Muhammad was born into one of the noble families of Mecca in the year 570 A.D. (53 years before the Hijrah, the Islamic calendar). His father's name was Abdullah, son of Abdul Mttalib of the tribe of Quraish and the clan of Hashim. His father died before Muhammad was born and was orphaned early. He was first raised and protected by his grandfather, Abdul Muttalib and after his grandfather's death by his uncle, Abu Talib.

As Muhammad was being raised by his uncle, Abu Talib, during the later period of his boyhood, he traveled with him, in Merchants' caravan to Syria. With the travel and trading experiences, Muhammad later on, was hired by a wealthy widow named Khadijah. He then made similar journeys to Syria in the services of Khadijah. Soon afterwards, she married her young agent who was fifteen years younger to her. This marriage gave him freedom of movement and time to think and develop his thoughts. This also gave him rank amongst the notables of Mecca.

Every year during the month of Ramadan, Muhammad would go with his family to the Mountain Hira. Here he would go for meditation in a cave. It was here, **when he was forty years old, towards the end of this quiet month of Ramadan, he had his first revelation.**

Muhammad's first convert was his wife Khadijah, his second convert was his cousin Ali and the third convert was his servant Zeyd. Among others, of his early converts were his old friend Abu Baker and some of his slaves and dependents. During first three years of his mission, Muhammad only preached to his family and to his intimate friends; the people of Mecca generally regarded him one who had become a little mad.

Then, at the end of the third year, Muhammad decided to present himself to the Meccans, in public, as the Prophet: the messenger of God. **He now preached openly against idolatry and the folly of worshiping many gods.** This angered Quraish who now became hostile to Muhammad's disciples; especially they began persecuting them. They even wanted to kill Muhammad but the blood- vengeance of Hashim clan, to which he belonged, prevented them from such action. His beliefs were so strong that he continued warning and threatening idolatrous about the consequences of "hell" and "burning in fire". In around 615 A.D., Muhammad sent his poor followers to Christian Abyssinia, thus protecting them from direct persecution.

Muhammad also convinced Jewish people that he was simply propagating their Scripture's message in Arabic language. On the other hand, he was sending the message to idol worshipers that those who disagreed with him were disbelievers and will be punished in the hell. Thus as the number of his followers increased, his opponents also became more bitter and determined. As opposition to Muhammad's teachings grew rigid, he, now, was having little success in converting the remaining population by preaching. He also made an attempt to preach to the inhabitants of Taif, a city east of Mecca, but was unsuccessful.

In the year 620 A.D., at the season of the yearly pilgrimage to Mecca, Muhammad met a group of men who heard him gladly. These men had come from Yathrib where learned Jewish rabbis had spoken to the pagans that an Arab Prophet will soon come. When these men met Muhammad, they recognized him as a prophet as the Jewish rabbis had told them. On their return to Yathrib, they relayed the information to their people; they told them all what they had seen and heard in Mecca. As a result, at the next season of pilgrimage, a deputation from Yathrib came to meet the Prophet and on meeting him they swore allegiance to him. Then they returned to Yathrib with a Muslim teacher.

In the following year (622 A.D.), seventy three Muslims from Yathrib came to Mecca to invite the Prophet to their city. This city was later named Al-Medinah, "the City" par excellence. It was then that the *Hijrah*, the flight to Yathrib was decided.

During this late Meccan period, prior to *Hijrah*, The Prophet had many revelations concerning God, his role, duty of the faithful and banning social ills. Some of which are, as follows:
- **I am the messenger of Allah,**
- **There is no God save Him,**
- **Pilgrimage to Mecca is a very important religious duty of the faithful,**

- **Rewards for being righteous and the believer are heaven, gardens enclosed and vineyards, and maidens for companions and full cup.**
- **Those who disbelieve, garment of fire will be cut out for them and boiling fluid will be poured down on their head.**

After about two years (between 620 A.D. and 622 A.D.) of negotiations with the representatives from Yathrib (Medina), Muhammad decided on *Hijrah* (migration to Medina). During this period, the Arab clans Aus and Khazraj of Medina had accepted Islam and the Jewish leaders had decided to help Muhammad.

With the decision on *Hijrah* made, the Muslims began selling their properties in Mecca and then leave for Medina. Abu Baker, Ali and the Prophet himself were last to leave Mecca. After traveling for many days, they reached Medina. Such was the flight of Muhammad from Mecca to Medina- the *Hijrah*, which counts the beginning of the Muslim era and is believed to correspond to July 16, 622 A.D.

To accomplish his goals, Muhammad needed the unified cooperation of the Meccan emigrants (*muhajirums*) and the Medinan "helpers" (*ansars*). Also to achieve his goal, in the first year of his reign at Medina, the Prophet also made treaty with the Jewish tribes. Having achieved social peace and cooperation from various factions in Medina, The Prophet now diverted his attention is obtaining more resources and in executing his plans. He decided to accomplish this goal by raiding Meccan caravans. In the second year of the Hijrah, as usual, the Meccan merchant caravan was returning from Syria and was to pass through the general area, close to Medina. The Prophet decided to capture the caravan. This was done at the "Battle of Badr" which was won by Muslims. This provided a prestige to Muhammad and weakened his opponents. After this he expelled the first of the three Jewish tribes and undecided Arabs accepted his faith.

Based on new revelations, Muslims were now commanded to:

- **Turn their face towards Kabah (at Mecca) in prayer,**
- **Fast during the month of Ramadan,**

- **Do not eat carrion, blood and swine-flesh, and**
- **Strong drinks and games of chance are forbidden.**

Now with the defeat at Badr, the Meccans had lost their prestige. In order to effectively carry out their foreign trade they needed to regain their lost prestige. Therefore, in the following year, (625 A.D.; 3 A.H.), Meccans mobilized a force of three thousand men and reached Uhud, which is located at the north-west border of Medina. During this battle, the Prophet received wounds. Following this, gathering around the Prophet, the Muslims retreated, leaving many dead. On the other hand, the Meccans were also exhausted in this battle. They felt that by wounding Muhammad they had taught a lesson to Muslims and it was of no use to fight anymore. The battle resulted in a status quo and provided opportunity to the prophet to reorganize and punish those he felt did not cooperate with him. His position was further strengthened when he forced the second Jewish tribe, the Banu Nadir, to emigrate and "winning the neutrals by intimidation".

In the battle of Uhud, many Muslims were killed. Since, in the pagan Arab world women had few rights, the concern for orphans and widows led to a declaration of some rights for women which they were deprived of earlier. Some of these, as mentioned in Surah 4, were, as follows:
- **Give unto orphans their wealth,**
- **Due to war time widowing of women, a man could marry up to four women, but only one if he fears that he can not do justice to them.**

In the year 627 A.D. (5 A.H.), with a force of about ten thousand men, Meccans advanced on Medina. The prophet mobilized a force of three thousand against Meccans. Meccans' numerical advantage was not as important as the strength of their cavalry. Their force was composed of Meccans and various other tribes. Therefore, they were not as cohesive and motivated as Muhammad's smaller but unified and well organized army. To contain Meccan's cavalry advantage, Muhammad took the advice of a Persian slave convert, Salman, and dug a ditch (Khandaq). This technique was new to Arabs and thus brought the cavalry to a virtual stand still; thus it is called the "Battle of the Ditch". Long waiting, followed by bitter winds blowing from the sea demoralized Meccan forces and they retired with minimal casualty to Muslims.

After the "Battle of Ditch", following the expulsion of all the three Jewish tribes from Medina and the acceptance of Islam by all Arab tribes, Medina now became a sovereign and homogeneous Islamic religious community. All the members of this community now accepted "adherence to God and his Prophet" and thus formed a Muslim community called *umma*. During the first month of the year 628 A.D. (6 A.H.), Muhammad took a "little pilgrimage" to Mecca. This pilgrimage (*Umra*) was taken with fifteen hundred volunteers. Most of the pilgrims were lightly armed and had taken with them sacrificial beasts. The Meccans became suspicious of their intentions and tried to stop Muhammad on his way. He, however, made to the boundary of haram at Al-Hudaibiya through another route and then initiated negotiations with Meccans. As a part of this negotiated settlement, the pilgrimage was declared to be completed. They, then, slaughtered the sacrificial beasts and returned back to Medina. The pilgrimage was duly completed in the following year.

By the end of the year 7 A.H. (629 A.D.), a large population of Mecca had either accepted Islam or became resigned to Muslim's power. In the following year 8 A.H.(630 A.D.), the Prophet organized a large force of all Muslims who were capable of bearing arms. After organizing this force, Prophet Muhammad marched to Mecca. The forces of Quraish, by now completely demoralized, put up token resistance to Muslim's attack. Therefore, the Prophet entered Mecca with his men almost without any resistance as a conqueror. After the complete victory of Mecca and the neighborhood, the Prophet returned to Al-Medinah. Then in the year 9 A.H. (631 A.D.), the Prophet had another revelation as recorded in Surah 9. That year the Prophet sent a message to the leader of the pilgrimage, Abu Bakr, which said that, "after that year Muslims only were to make pilgrimage,----." That proclamation actually ended idol-worship in Arabia.

In the year 10 A.H. (632 A.D.), the Prophet went to Mecca as a pilgrim for the last time. Soon after his return from the pilgrimage, in the year 10 A.H. (632 A.D.), the prophet fell sick and after a short illness, he died on June 6,632 A.D., 10 A.H.

Thus, the Prophet, the warner and the messenger, preached the existence of one and the only one God through a series of revelations. He also established a religious-political community of Islam based on equality among its followers. This community, within a very short period of time, after his death, expanded fast and became a very powerful force.

5

RAAM

5.1 INDIAN SUBCONTINENT BEFORE RAAM AND HIS BIRTH

Indian Subcontinent & the Society Prior to Raam

As shown in **Figure 5 .1**, the Indian subcontinent where Raam was born and preached is over 2000 miles long and about 1500 miles wide. Its climate varies from snow capped Himalayan Mountains to the vast Indo-Gangatic valley in the north to the southern plateau and the western Thaar Desert. At the time of Raam, the subcontinent had vast forests with multitudes of plants, trees and vegetation and various kinds of wildlife. Then and as now, the land had numerous rivers, streams and water bodies. The society had well settled villages, towns and cities. They were administered by village Panchayats (five elected people), local chieftains, kings (*raja*) and then the emperor (*Chkravarti raja* or the *Maharaja*). A large group of the people also liked to live in the woods and had their semi-autonomous tribal chiefs who in turn were under the local king. The society was primarily agricultural. The land was rich, therefore, common man had plentiful of everything. The result was that the masses had enough time to think, discuss and ponder about the purpose of life, the existence of God, human welfare and the culture.

Indian philosophy, theology and culture had evolved over many thousands of years before Raam was born. In general, everybody living in the subcontinent followed the same Dharm but had numerous Ways of Worship, each to his or her interest, liking and/or upbringing.

Dharm means duty: In general, the Dharm of every Indian (here I mean the person living in the Indian subcontinent) was to follow the following main tenets:

- Honor thy father, mother, guru (teacher) and elders.
- Have mutual love, respect and trust between you and your spouse and both men and women must be monogamous.
- Engage in actions that will lead to the betterment of the weak and the poor.
- Get away from *Kam* (lust), *Krodh* (anger), *Lobh* (greed), *Moh* (wordly attachment), *Muthe* (intoxication), and *Matsarya* (jealousy).
- Love, value and protect human life.
- Respect all ways of worship to God.

Thus Dharm was a kind of "the Law of the Land".

Freedom for the Ways of Worship: All ways of worship to God were to be respected and valued. The theology had evolved to the level that it was generally accepted that various paths can lead to the Kingdom of God. The human travel of life was compared to the flow of rivers that traversed different paths but in the end lead to the same vast body of water, the ocean. Similarly, it was argued that, for humans, different ways of worship to the same almighty God will eventually lead one to the same God.

Thus, every Indian had to follow the same Dharm but could have different ways of worship; this is a kind of separation of "church and the state". This meant that in the same town, village and the family people could follow different ways of worship but would adhere to the same Dharm.This later,

Figure 5.1 The Indian Subcontinent Where Raam was Born
(Base Map: Courtesy of The General Libraries UT at Austin, 2003)

inappropriately, was named by outsiders as the Hindu religion. This is because that the people living outside the larger Indian subcontinent (from the present day Afganistan to the borders of Burma (or Mayamar)) observed that people living around the River Sindhu (Sindh) and east of it, all lived by the same tenets (social laws) or Dharm. So they called them Sindus or Hindus (Iranians would substitute H for S in their pronunciation). They did not understand that Indians kept the state laws and the way of worship separate. So irrespective of their way of worship people living in the larger Indian subcontinent, around the River Sindh or east of it, were called Hindus and the religions (ways of worship) of all these people was understood to be one and the same, thus named Hindu.

The wise men and the sages of the time in the land would generally preach to the masses that they should worship God, follow Dharm and have the following key goals for their lives:

- *Karam* (work)
- *Arth* (collection and utilization of material goods)
- *Dhyan* (In the process always remember God).
- *Moksh* (follow Dharm so that one can attain heaven).

Indian Society at the Time of Raam's Birth

At the time Raam was born, cracks had already developed in the society based on theology and the social status. Although the land was rich and fertile, generally masses were well off and were being ruled by their own people, **great divisions between the people** based on their **ways of worship and social status** were quite evident throughout the land. A major class divide had also developed between the rulers and the ruled as well as between the city and town dwellers and the forest (wood) dwellers. There were many social and political leaders who were **not following what they**

were preaching. For example, according to Dharm you are supposed to obey your father but many people would only selectively follow this, i.e., only when it appeared to be for their benefit. Similarly, every one who opted to be married was required to be monogamous, but many people in power would not follow this tenant of Dharm.

From the ways of worship point of view, there were three main denominations that began to preach that theirs was the best way of worship. These were:
- Vishnu followers,
- Shiv followers, and
- The followers of the God of Vedic Tradition (as expounded in Vedas and Upnishads).

There was a great debate across the land and in the entire society about the supremacy and even the truthfulness and the existence of ones way of worship to the God. Although all these denominations propagated that their interpretation of the God was omnipotent and omnipresent, Vishnu and Shiv followers believed that the God can only take the form of their definition of God. The God of Vedic Tradition, however, in addition to being compassionate, omnipotent and omnipresent was also indivisible, infinite and invisible. These different denominations now instead of respecting each others way of worship would many times insult other ways of worship. Although, most of these denominations were generally vocal about expressing the superiority of their way of worship, they however, would not use force to convince others to follow their way of worship.

On the contrary, a large and powerful group of people, called **Rakshash, were forcibly imposing their way of worship** on others **and openly disregarding the principles of Dharm**. Their life style, primarily, was based on the philosophy of "eat, drink and be merry". In leading this life style, they would harm others, steal and acquire forcefully what was others' and openly went against the ways of Dharm. Their sinful acts would cause major pain and suffering among the common masses, especially those in the weaker sections of the population. Protectors of the society were so much afraid of these sinners that instead of protecting the weak and the poor they would make alliances with these wrong doers so that their kingdom and privileged lives were protected.

Raam's Parents and His Birth

In the city of Ayodhya, capital of the Kingdom of Koshal, situated on the banks of River Saryu, in the Indo-Gangatic valley, a king named Dashrath reigned. He was renowned, powerful, righteous and wise. He was a sincere devotee of Vishnu but he respected all other ways of worship. He followed Dharm. He, however, did not follow one tenant of Dharm which was "both men and women must be monogamous." He married three wives. The king was in his advanced age but still did not have a child. One day king Dashrath went to his *guru* (teacher), Vasishth, and related to him his reason for sadness; which was that even at this older age he did not have a child. Hearing this, the *guru* invited a learned sage, named Shringi, who performed a special prayer to the God. The sage then prepared a special food mixed with herbs that had fertility medicinal effects. He then instructed the king to give the food to his three queens whose names were Kaushalya, Kaikeyi and Sumitra. After eating this medicinal food, prepared in the presence of the holy spirit of God, the queens eventually became pregnant.

It was the ninth day of the first month of Indian calendar, the month of Chaitr (late March-early April), the moon was on the rising cycle and the spring weather was on, when queen Kausalya felt happiness and was filled with spiritual peace. She experienced the presence of God. She then began worshiping the God with her folded hands and said, "O infinite Lord, how may I praise you? The Vedas and the Puranas declare you beyond illusion, attributes and knowledge, and immeasurable. He whom the Vedas and holy men hymn as the ocean of mercy and bliss and repository of all virtues, the same lord of Laxmi who loves his votaries, has revealed himself for my weal" (Balkand : 2). When she was in a deep meditating stage she heard the baby's delightful sound and came out of her spiritual meditation; it was the crying sound of her new born baby Raam who had just been born to her. Soon other queens also gave birth to their lovely sons. It was a joyful occasion for all the citizens and they all celebrated it with great happiness. On an auspicious day, in accordance with the holy tradition of *Nam Sanskar* (naming ceremony), they were named Raam, Bharat, Laxman and Shatrughan.

Education and Apprenticeship

Raam and his brothers grew up with other children of their age in a normal way. He was always a delight to his parents, relatives and neighbors. All those associated with him enjoyed his company. As the brothers grew up, in accordance with the tradition, they were sent to their *guru's* (teacher's) educational institution. Raam learnt all the disciplines of education including theology and the art of using arms. He "became proficient in scholarship and modesty and virtue and decorum and practiced all princely sports." The gracious behavior of all four brothers, such as being respectful to elders and treating their peers as equals, made citizens love them dearer than their own lives. With time, Raam became an expert archer, and mastered war techniques. He also became well versed in *Vedas*, *Upnishads*, theology, administration and philosophy.

A sage named Vishwamitra (meaning a friend of the entire world) lived in his *Ashram* (modest residence in the forest) where he practiced *yog* (yoga), practiced meditation, preached to who ever came to hear him and worshiped the God of Vedas (indivisible and invisible one God). There were some people with Satanic and Devilish philosophy, who did not like this way of worship and philosophy. Two leaders of these people named Marich and Subahu, would come and threaten the sage and his followers. They would destroy their places of worship and attack them. Sage Vishwamitra came to king Dashrath and asked him to send Raam and his brother Laxman to protect his Ashram. Dashrath was saddened because he did not want to be away from his son, Raam, who in his early twenties, was still young for such a task. He said to the sage that he will send a big army to protect him. The sage knew that only Raam could protect him. Therefore he was insistent on having Raam to come and protect his Ashram. Although king Dashrath's way of worship was to follow God Vishnu and sage Vishwamitra was a follower of the God of Vedas, the Dharm of a king required that he **protect all his citizens irrespective of their way of worship**. Realizing this, Raam and Dashrath consulted their *guru* Vasishth and the king, in spite of all the dangers for his sons' life, agreed to send Raam and Laxman with the sage.

Raam and Laxman, following the path of Dharm, accompanied the sage to his Ashram. There they further learnt the theology of Vedas and the God. They also learnt survival techniques and obtained the knowledge about various herbs and their medicinal powers. As they lived in the Ashram, away from the luxuries of the urban living, they also learnt about the ways many people in the kingdom lived. They protected the sage's worship place, his preaching assemblies and his way of worship. Many a times they had to fight those who would not listen to the reason and would not respect different ways of worship. They had to engage in many battles to protect the sage and his followers. In the end, they were successful in their mission and defeated the evil forces. It should be noted that everybody, if possible, would fight to protect themselves and sometimes would fight to protect the people of their own faith but rarely people would defend the persons of different faith. Raam, on other hand, fought to protect others who had different way of worship than his. Since this was the first time, after completing his education in his guru's institute, that Raam by himself fought wars to protect righteous people, it was a sort of apprenticeship for him. In this mission he **protected the weak and fought to keep the freedom of worship for others**. This was a selfless and holy mission of Dharm.

Raam Visited a Lonely Hermitage: Respect and Equality for Women

One day sage Vishwamitra told Raam to accompany him to witness the "ceremony of the contest of the bow" in the kingdom of King Janak (situated in the present day Bihar province). This ceremony was arranged by Janak as a part of *Swayamber* (ceremony of selecting ones own husband), which was a tradition for the selection of a groom by the bride among those invited in the ceremony. In this ceremony, the bride had a free choice to garland the person of her liking who she would then marry. In some cases, certain conditions for the selection of the groom, among the attendees, were also outlined. In this specific case, Sita, King Janak's daughter and her father had agreed that Sita would only marry a person who would have mastered the art of archery. This became especially important to both Sita and her father because Sita herself was fond of archery and a few years earlier she herself had drawn a special bow with ease. Therefore they both set the test condition which was that the person should be able to lift and draw this special bow originally belonging to a master archer, who was God Shiv's follower. The bow was very heavy, was specially made with a long range and required a skillful and strong person to draw it. Both Raam and Laxman accompanied the sage to take part in this ceremony. On the way to the ceremony, they saw a hermitage devoid of any sign of life or any activity. A lady, named Ahilya, was residing there and was leading a secluded life. She was so quiet and lived a very monotonous and almost static life that it would appear as if she was a stone. No one visited her and she led the life of an outcast. When asked about the situation, the sage told the story as follows.

Vishwamitra said that some time ago, a sage named Gautam lived here with his young and beautiful wife Ahilya. Once his friend King Indr, came to the Ashram very early in the morning when it was dark and he knew that the sage was out of his residence. Indra changed his appearance and the voice and made it look and sound similar to that of the sage. Ahilya, who was still sleeping, could not distinguish this disguise, especially in the dark. Indr, then tricked her in having sex with him. When the sage came to know about it, he penalized Indr and left his wife. Indr later repented, went through a sever penance and was rehabilitated by the society. However, neither the sage nor the society would forgive Ahilya who was tricked into the act and did it unknowingly. In addition she also went through severe penance. Ever since this unfortunate occurrence, she led the life of an outcast. She repented, prayed regularly to God and even though it was not her fault she begged for forgiveness. But she was permanently penalized. Hearing this story, Raam's heart was filled with sadness and sympathy. He realized the unfair treatment Ahilya received just because she was a woman. He felt that this was a discriminatory, deceitful and sinful behavior of the society and decided to correct the wrong done to the innocent lady. Raam, accompanied by the sage and his followers, went to the lonely hermitage, touched Ahilya with affection, talked to her and made her feel again a part of the society. He consoled her and gave her honor and respect a fellow human deserves. Observing Raam's compassionate and fair action, people, from that day on, also happily accepted Ahilya in the society. This bold and compassionate behavior of Raam exhibited his **respect for women and treating them on equal footing similar to men.** Although people with wicked thought would still criticize Raam but a majority of the people, especially with pure soul, praised Raam for his being "such a great friend of the humble and so causelessly compassionate." His followers then decided to "**give up all entanglements of deceit**" (Balkand: 211).

5.2 RAAM'S MARRIAGE AND HIS LEAVING THE PALACE: OPTS OUT TO LIVE WITH THE POOR AND THE WEAK

After meeting and reinstating Ahilya's honor, Raam, with the sage and accompanied by their followers, continued the journey to the city of Janakpuri, the capital of King Janak. On reaching the city they observed that the city was clean with well kept gardens, well laid out streets and crossings, and had beautiful markets and all the shops were filled with all sorts of goods. Above all the citizens were courteous, well educated, God fearing and kept away from their sins. The king had strong army with numerous horses, elephants and chariots. After settling down in a place where the king had made arrangements for their stay, Raam and Laxman with the permission of the sage, went to see the city. Both Raam and Laxman were so handsome, strong and well behaved that the citizens very quickly developed affection for them. In addition, as the word spread about Raam's good deeds of defeating the evil spirited people and protecting Vishwamitr's Ashram from Satanic peoples' evil acts and rehabilitating Ahilya in the society, the crowds began coming to see Raam in large numbers. All citizens wished if Raam could win the contest and Sita could select and marry such a handsome, fair-minded and pious leader who also has a pure soul. After meeting with the people and seeing the beautiful city, both Raam and Laxman, returned to their place of stay.

Raam Meets Sita & Marrys Her

Next morning, Raam and Laxman went to the beautiful public garden to fetch flowers for their *guru's* Morning Prayer ceremony. As they were obtaining permission from the gardener to pluck the flowers, Sita also came there to get flowers for her mother's Morning Prayer ceremony. Although both Ram and Sita had heard about each other and were familiar with their characteristics and abilities, they had never met before. But now after meeting for the first time, they both fell in love at the first site. After some formal introduction and communication they both returned to their respective residences.

At the scheduled time both Raam and Laxman went to the arena where the ceremony of the bow was being held. It was a very large theater and separate seating arrangements were made for the contestants, courtiers, priests, sages and hermits, and the citizens. The arena was completely full. Then Sita accompanied by her escorts came and took her seat. She was very beautiful and everybody was fascinated by her charm. Then one by one the contestants came on the stage and tried to lift the bow and then draw it with the arrow. Some of them even could not lift it. Others who could lift it could not draw it. Those who could lift and draw the bow could not aim the arrow with it. Raam being the youngest came last. He easily picked it up, drew it and accurately aimed with the arrow. His aim was accurate and he pulled it with such strength that after discharging the arrow it broke into pieces. Raam was the winner. Sita was very happy and she picked up the garland and placed it around Raam's neck indicating that she accepted Raam as her husband. All the citizens were very happy. The wedding ceremony was appropriately completed. The whole city was filled with happiness and the celebratory atmosphere was all over in the kingdom.

The following is a chronology of Raam, from his birth to his marriage:
- King **Dashrath** had four sons: **Raam**, Laxman, Bharat and Shatrughan
- Raam's childhood *guru*(teacher) was **Vasishth**
- Raam's adulthood teacher was **Vishwamitra**
- Raam married **Sita**, daughter of king Janak

Raam Again Fights to Retain the Freedom of Worship

Raam came from the family who worshiped God in the form of Vishnu while Sita's family worshiped God in the form of Shiv. Sages, like Vishwamitra, generally worshiped the God of Vedas (one, indivisible, invisible, compassionate and merciful God). According to the tenants of Indian Dharm everyone had a right to follow the way of worship of their choice. However, some Shiv followers, with fundamentalist theology, did not like the marriage between two people with different way of worship although as in the past this has been an acceptable practice. They disapproved this marriage and were ready to fight. Raam, Sita,Vishwamitra, Janak and citizens did not like this intolerance. First both Raam and Laxman tried to convince the fundamentalists by reason and citing scriptures and the words of many wise men about the Dharm. Hearing this, a large number of people realized their mistake and accepted the way of Dharm. However, even after trying their hard, they could not convince some die-hard fundamentalists who challenged them for a battle. Raam, although a strong and fearless fighter, did not want such an unnecessary bloodshed. He repeatedly tried to reason with them. In the end Raam and Laxman reluctantly agreed for the battle. As preparation for the battle began it became quite clear that a majority of the fighters (who were followers of Vishnu, Shiv and God of Vedas) and all the citizens came on Raam's side. This was because all of them understood that it was sinful to force one's way of worship on others and everybody had a right to follow their way of worship. Realizing that they will not win, the disheartened fundamentalists with anti-Dharm philosophy withdrew their opposition to this wedding and went home disheartened. One of these people was Ravan, the king of Lanka (the island kingdom of the present day Shri Lanka).

Raam Opts Out to Live in the Forest for Fourteen Years

After Raam and Sita's wedding, in due course, his brothers also got married. This made their father very happy and he thanked God for giving him a prosperous and happy family. Then the king, with the permission of his guru and agreement with his five counselors (called Punch) began preparations to invest Raam with regal powers. Hearing this news all the citizens were delighted; they were eagerly waiting for such an auspicious occasion. They all began talking about it and in their conversations they all agreed that Raam would be an ideal king. They knew that Raam was compassionate, fair to all, respected all humans equally, believed in treating all faiths equally, was a learned man, was well versed in theology as well as in the military techniques, was free of all sins and was dedicated to God and the tenants of Dharm.

Hearing that Raam would now become the King of Ayodhya, wise men and sages of the land assembled and realized that such a great man with godly qualities is needed to preach and protect the weak and the poor outside the cities and the towns. They realized that until this work was completed the kingdom's work could be supervised by his younger brother Bharat who was an able administrator, was of pure soul and was dedicated to his elder brother Raam. They prayed to God to help them in this effort. God then commanded king's favorite queen Kakayi to convince king Dashrath to send Raam for fourteen years in the forest. Although Kakayi knew that neither the king nor the public will like this suggestion she followed God's instructions because she was convinced that this action would be for greater good of the society. She talked to the king and insisted that he should send Raam to forest for fourteen years and in the meantime her son Bharat should be the king. She even reminded the king that in the past he had promised her to fulfill her one wish which she was asking to give her now. King Dashrath was famous for keeping his word. So he was in a precarious situation now. Although the old king would not accept the proposal of sending Raam to the forest but now under these circumstances he did not know what to do. This, however, pained him and he became ill. After knowing all this the great soul Raam went to his father and volunteered to go to forest for the prescribed time period. This he did to keep his father's word and to serve humanity as understood by sages and commanded by God. Raam then talked to his father, consoled him and said that he will be back soon. He said to his father, "Blessed is his life upon this earth whose father is pleased to hear of his doings. The four rewards of life, (viz., religious merit, material riches, sensuous gratification and final beatitude), are within his grasp who loves his parents as he loves his own life" (Ayodhyakand :45-1).

After saying good bye to his parents, guru and the citizens Raam, accompanied by his brother, Laxman and wife Sita left for the forest. In the beginning he tried to convince both Sita and Laxman not to accompany him because he understood that he was opting for a hard life and did not want them to go through such hardships. However, both of them loved him and his cause so much that they refused to stay back. Finally, Raam out of his great love for them relented and they accompanied him. Many people could not accept this so they tried to convince Raam not to go. Many of them even followed him for a long distance and kept on asking him to change his mind.

Even though Raam knew that he will have to lead a hard and dangerous life in the woods, for the sake of the weak, poor, and the unprotected folks and to protect the Dharm, he left his comfortable life behind and went to live with the poor. Such sacrifice without a hitch could only be done by a holy soul with a mission to serve God which meant serving the outcast, weak and the meek.

Meeting Nishadraj & Forest Dwellers : Common Masses & the sages

Then Raam moved ahead on his journey to the forest. The leader of a tribe, named Guha (lovingly called Nishadraj) living in the Vindhya Mountains, heard that Raam was coming in his direction; hearing this he was delighted. During that time agriculture was considered the best profession for a common man. Tribal people did not engage in agriculture but followed other trades such as boat transportation, wood cutting and other related trades. His profession and the profession of his tribal people, as a whole, were not given due respect in the society. Raam was against this discrimination and had spoken numerous times against this practice. Nishadraj had heard of Raam's progressive, humanitarian and God-loving teaching as was related to him by hermits and sages. He came and greeted Raam, accorded him due respect as he entered in his territory. Raam embraced him and addressed him as a "wise friend." He thanked Guha for his kind hospitality, love and trust. He then advised Nishadraj and his people to **be proud of their profession, heritage and the way of worship and follow the path of Dharm**. He said that **in God's eyes all humans are equal**. Raam then assured them that he with God's blessings will protect them against any injustices as long as they followed Dharm.

Raam then moved on, visiting sages, people of other tribes and holy places respected by the people of different faiths in the land. He worshiped God, the almighty, in all those places of worship. Away from the luxuries of the palace, he, Sita and Laxman were now sleeping on the ground, wearing rough clothes, and eating roots, forest fruits and the food of a common man of the area they would visit. In the process they became a part of the masses. As they would come near a village, large crowds would come to see and hear Raam. In the holy city of Prayag (present day city of Allahabad) religious students, ascetics, hermits, adepts and recluses all came to see and hear him. He would teach them to keep away from their sins and follow the path of Dharm. His key message was, **"Until a man is unfeignedly devoted to God in thought and word and deed, he cannot even dream of happiness, despite all that he may do"** (Ayodhyakand : 107).

Then Raam came to the Ashram of sage Valmiki. Although Valmiki had achieved many successes by mastering theology, meditation, serving, teaching, preaching and leading a pious life, his past still haunted him. This is because originally he came from a very humble background and turned to be a common criminal and bandit. Eventually, he changed, turned away from his sins and now for a very long period of time was leading a very pious and saintly life. Even many of his learned colleagues would not fully accept him as their equal. Raam did not like this. **He did not believe in a person's past. He would value a person for what he or she is now** and his promise for his way of living and acting for the future. Therefore, Raam intentionally came to Valmiki's Ashram. He addressed Valmiki as "O king of sages" and in the presence of other sages and followers accorded him due respect. Following this, in Valmiki's Ashram, in the presence of Raam, teachings and preaching of the scriptures were presented to all attendees. These were as follows:

- God is the custodian of the universe and is beyond the range of speech and reason, is incomprehensible, infinite and is as described in Vedas as "Not thus, not thus."
- God dwells in the heart of those who have no lust or anger, arrogance, pride or infatuation, are without greed, excitement, attraction or aversion and who are free from hypocrisy.
- God is pleased with those who look upon other person's wife as their own mother.
- The salvation is for those who rejoice to see others' prosperity and feel distressed at their misfortune and help them with all of their energies.

After these teachings and preaching, Raam moved on and eventually, made a hut on the Chitrakut Mountain and made this place his residence.

Here, he made friendship with the tribes of Kole, Bheel, and Kirats. He preached among them, taught them the practical ways of life, in addition to what they knew and made them aware of the way of Dharm. He also stressed that they should be proud of their way of life but should always keep away from sinful actions. He became their friend, advisor, and protector. As time passed, many sages, wise men and common folks from villages and towns came to see and hear Raam at the Chitrakut Mountaian. He preached among all and helped the weak; he also stressed the need for coexistence between people of different life styles.

Younger Brother Bharat and Raam Meet

After Raam settled down on the Chitrakut Mountain to live with the locals, Dashrath's chief counselor, Sumantr, who opted to accompany Raam so far, realized that he had done his best to try to bring Raam back to Ayodhya prior to fourteen years. It became clear to him that Raam was determined to work with the people for full fourteen years as promised. When Sumantr was departing, he asked Raam for advice to be given to the citizen's and his family. In response, Raam said, to please take his salutation to his parents and elders, and love to the younger generation. He also said that when Bharat returns back, after visiting our relatives, give him this advice, " Abandon not the path of rectitude when you ascend the thrown; cherish your subjects in thoughts and word and deed, and serve each queen mother with equal respect." With these words Sumantr returned to Ayodhya. After knowing that Raam did not return, Dashrath got into deep sadness and died.

When Bharat returned from his relative's place he was told all what had happened. Instead of being delighted for being given the throne and on the occasion of his coronation as the king of Ayodhya, Bharat as a God fearing, follower of the tenants of Dharm and an ideal brother was greatly pained and saddened. He refused to accept the throne and said that the throne only belonged to no one else but to his elder brother Raam only. He decided to go the forest, meet Raam and bring him back. He also promised that if Ram would not come back due to his resolve to live and work with the locals in the forest he, Bharat, would stay in the forest in place of Raam. With such a resolve, Bharat began his journey to the forest. Hearing this, many citizens, counselors and people of various positions accompanied Bharat to bring Raam back to the palace.

On Bharat's arrival at the Chitrakut Mountain hut, Raam greeted Bharat with affection and advised him to go back and take care of his duties as a king. Bharat, various ministers, and *guru* Vasishth, tried different arguments but could not convince Raam to come back. He felt strongly on his promise to his father and the sages that he will live and work with the people of the land and the forests for fourteen years. After realizing that Raam would not return until he had finished his mission, Bharat took leave from Raam, returned to Ayodhya, built a hut for him outside the city and resolved to lead the life of ascetics, similar to that of Raam. From there he administered the protection of the land, received all his advisors and periodically gave them appropriate instructions. He delegated the work of justice, treasury, education and welfare to his *guru* who the family trusted the most. All the government work was then done by the ministers under the guidance of *guru* Vashisth. All the work of the Kingdom was done in the name of Raam which exhibited the dedication and the respect for Raam by all.

5.3 REACHING OUT AND HELPING THE FOREST DWELLERS

Then Raam continued his work among the tribal people, villagers and sages. He protected them all based on their needs. For example, tribal people needed education, self respect and self reliance, and the protection of their rights as equal citizens in the land. The villagers needed education, reminder of the tenants of Dharm, and sages needed the protection to perform their worships, meditation and the freedom to spread the word of God. After Bharat came to Chitrakut Mountain with his ministers and citizens, Raam realized that he will keep on receiving royal visitors; this he understood will come on his way in dedicating full time to the service of the people. Therefore, he decided to move to some other location where he could do his work without interruption. So Raam, Sita and Laxman, bade farewell to the place.

Mutual Respect Between Raam & the Sages

From the Chitrakut Mountain, Raam went to the hermitage of sage Atri. Hearing that a great soul like Raam had come to his hermitage, the great sage Atri was delighted and rushed to greet him. He then escorted Raam to his place of worship; they both then worshiped together and then thanked the Almighty for giving them chance to serve the humanity of His creation. The sage Atri admired Raam's mission and sacrifices he was making in order to perform God's work. Atri continued saying that both Raam and he should work together for the good of the humanity and spread the good word of the omnipotent, eternal transcending, the one absolute Lord and serve Him in the form of humanity. When Raam and Atri were discussing theology and their ways of serving God, Sita and sage Atri's wife, Anasuya, began their discussions on Dharm and their role in the missions of their husbands.

The sage lady, Ansuya, being older and more experienced in the world said, "Fortitude, piety, a friend and a wife – these four are tested only in time of adversity." They both talked about the mission Raam had undertaken and agreed that it could not be completed without Sita's full cooperation and support. They also talked about the need for dedication of a husband and his wife for one another both in their thoughts and deeds. After some rest, Sita, Raam and Laxman took permission from the sage and moved on.

As Raam, Sita and Laxman traveled throughout the land they met many people and continued preaching the good ways of Dharm. Many dedicated workers of the God also joined them on their mission. As he walked with his followers Raam also witnessed piles of human skeletons that Rakshashas (people with demonic philosophy) had left after killing the pro-Dharm people. This saddened Raam greatly.

Raam met and preached among the sages including learned and pious sages like Sharbhang, Sutikshn, and the great seer Agusutay and promised them protection from evil Rakshashas. Finally, Raam with his disciples reached Panchvati. There he met Gidhraj who was the leader of a tribe who lived very primitive life. Their food habits and the way of living could be compared with vultures. He became Raam's friend and promised to change his ways and follow the path of Dharm. He then helped Raam and Laxman build a hut near the River Godavari in Panchavati. Raam, Sita and Laxman, then, settled there and made it their residence. Now, all sages and God loving and Dharm following people felt safe and were delighted with the presence of Raam in their community. Rakshashs, however, were unhappy and angry because now they could not do sinful acts without the fear of being punished by Raam. Also, they now could not force their only way of worship and anti-Dharm way of life on others without being resisted.

Further Preaching & Spreading God's Message

One time, Raam was sitting among his disciples. Laxman, then asked him about "*Gyan* (spiritual wisdom), *Waragya* (dispassion) *Maya* (illusion) and *Bhaki* (devotion)." Raam said that (1) **Spiritual Wisdom** is that which makes one free from all blemishes, such as, false pride, and which sees Absolute equality among all things, (2) A man of supreme **Dispassion** is one who has abandoned all psychic powers (*Sidhi* or Perfection) and all material goods, (3) The sense of " I" and "Mine", "You" and "Yours" is **Illusion** which holds sway over all individuals, and (4) **Devotion** to God, Almighty, is when one gets away from all sins and leads a righteous life. God is at the command of the votary who "observes the strict rule of prayer and praise, in thought and word and deed; who recognizes none but God as his guru, father, mother, brother, spouse, and all, and is steadfast in God's service" (Arayankand : 15- 5).

Raam further said that God loves those who in word, thought and deed worship Him without the expectation of any reward. He continued by saying, "O brother! there are three evils most formidable of all- lust, wrath and greed." The power of greed lies in desire and vanity. The power of lust lies in sexual attraction of a man to a woman and a woman to a man. Finally, the power of wrath lies in harsh speech. Raam then concluded that blessed are those who "**have conquered the six passions (lust, anger, greed, infatuation, false pride and jealousy); are sinless, disinterested, firm, possessing nothing, pure (both within and without), full of bliss, of boundless wisdom, desireless, truthful, inspired, scholarly and disciplined**" (Arayandkand : 44-4).

With these words Raam concluded by stressing that one must follow the path of Dharm and worship the God all times in thoughts and deeds. He preached that the **simplest way to realize the kingdom of God is through Devotion (*Bhakti*), leading a Sinless (*Nishpap*) life, Service (doing good to others), and Dharm.**

Rakshs' First Attack : Sages Protected

When Rakshashs realized that Raam now had a large following among the sages, villagers and the tribal people and they all were now leading the path of Dharm, they first wanted to discredit Raam. So they sent, Supernakha, a beautiful lady, to trap Raam in her prangs of love. Supernakha was the sister of Ravan, the King of Lanka and the leader of Rakshashs. She came to the area where Raam was preaching and serving the people. She first tried to entrap Raam and then Laxman by making lustful suggestions and love entrapment. But she was totally unsuccessful in her evil motives. Then frustrated Surparnakha attacked Sita. Laxman then defended Sita from the attack of the evil Supernakha. In this process, Supernakha received some injuries on her face. She then went crying to local Rakshash chiefs, Khar and Dushan. They came with a very strong, well equipped and large army of fighters to attack Raam. Their goal was to defeat Raam and then further degrade the dharma followers by abducting Sita. Raam, first tried to reason with them and tried to tell them that it is against Dharm to play prangs of love and lust with a married person and then attack his wife. He said that one should treat his wife and also other person's wife with respect. Rakshashs, who always had evil mind, did not even want to hear such words. They attacked Raam and his followers. In defence, Raam, Laxman and his followers counter-attacked the evil forces. Although, Raam and his followers were fewer in numbers, they had God on their side. A major battle ensued. In the end Rakshashs were defeated and their survivors ran away. Raam let them go because he would "never kill an enemy in retreat." This retreat of Rakshashs made sages and the God fearing people feel safe. They now could follow the righteous path freely.

Abduction of Sita by Rakshashs' Emperor Ravan

Perceiving the destruction of Khar and Dushan, Surpanakha went to her powerful brother Ravan and told him that the power of Rakshashs is declining and one day he will also lose everything if he did not act on time. She told him how Raam's followers of Dharm are increasing in numbers and strength. Hearing this, Ravan decided to tackle Raam himself since Ravan was both physically and strategically strong. He, however, realized that in spite of his personal strength he would not be able to win in a direct fight with Raam. So he decided to follow an evil trick. He first went to Mareech, one of his staunch followers, a master in disguise and a fast runner; he also knew the terrain well. Ravan, therefore, asked Mareech to disguise in the form of a beautiful deer and to go in front of Raam's hut. When Sita saw this exquisitely ravishing deer from a distance, she requested Raam to get that deer's skin. First Raam tried to convince her against it but when she insisted, Raam went for hunting. At that time Raam warned his brother,

Laxman, against the evil spirited Rakshashs and told him to protect the residence. After chasing the deer for a long distance, Raam shot it. As was planned by Ravan, when Mareech was shot with the arrow he screamed with a painful voice: Laxman, Laxman. Hearing this, Sita thought that Raam was in trouble so she forced Laxman to go and help Raam who she thought was in trouble. Laxman reluctantly went in the direction where the distress voice came. Ravan in the guise of a sage went to Sita's residence and asked for alms, which many hermits would do since they did not own anything and spent most of their time in meditation and preaching. As soon as Sita opened the door to give alms to Ravan, who was in the guise of a hermit, he revealed his real form and then forcibly abducted her in his chariot. Sita shouted for help. When Jatayu, the vulture tribe chief, came to protect her Ravan killed him with his sword. Ravan then took her to Lanka and put her below an Ashoka tree in his garden. He then tried every kind of threat and punishment to make her agree to marry him. Since Raam was preaching to the masses that everyone must have one wife and respect other person's wife like his own mother, Ravan wanted to show them the opposite path; that too by force. This was unlike Raam who was preaching, the path of Dharm, with love.

Meeting with Sabari : An Old tribal Woman

When Raam and Laxman returned, Jatayu who was on his death bed told them the whole story and how Ravan forcefully abducted Sita and how he unsuccessfully fought him. Raam was greatly saddened. After performing Jatayu's last rights, Raam and Laxman proceed in search of Sita. On their way, Raam visited Shabari's hermitage. Shabari was an old woman of Shavari tribe. Generally, people would consider below their dignity to visit and have a meal with a poor, old and illiterate tribal woman. Recognizing this wrong tradition, which he had been preaching was a great sin; Raam made it a point to visit her. He then had a meal with her and praised her for her life long pious deeds and always keeping away from sins. When she thanked Raam for visiting a person who is "lowest of the low", Raam replied that **God recognizes no relationship except that of faith** which she had. Raam then preached about the value of faith by saying, " Despite social class, kinship, lineage, piety, reputation, wealth, power, connections, accomplishments and ability, **a man without faith is of no more account than a cloud without water**" (Arayanyakand :34-3).

Raam then told Shabari, the **nine types of devotions**, as follows:
- Fellowship with saints,
- Fondness for the legends relating to God,
- Selfless service,
- Hymning of all God's virtues with a guileless heart,
- Repetition of God's mystic Name with steadfast faith,
- The practice of self-governance and virtue,
- See the entire world equally,
- Be content with whatever one has, and
- Be simple and cherish implicit faith in God without exultation or depression.

Then Raam said, "O lady, very dear to me; you have them all in the highest degree."

5.4 RAAM TEACHES VARIOUS LEADERS THE PATH OF DHARM AND DEATH OF EVIL RAVAN

Raam Meets Hanuman and Sugreev

Then Raam and Laxman proceeded further in search of Sita and arrived near the hills of Rishyamuk. There they met Sugreev and his minister Hanuman. Hanuman had heard about the great deeds and God loving behavior of Raam. When he was introduced to Raam in person, Hanuman was very happy. He found the great soul of Raam, in person, even more impressive. When Hanuman asked about the reason for their coming to the area, Raam told him the whole story and said that they were searching for Sita who had been forcibly abducted by Ravan. Although Hanuman had never met Raam, he had always respected and loved him for his sacrifices and for leading humanity on the path of Dharm. Now after meeting Raam, Hanuman's life dream was completed and he instantly dedicated his life in his services. Then Sugreev told his story to Raam. He said that his brother, Bali, originally a Dharm follower has now abandoned Dharm and is following Ravan's philosophy of anti-Dharm. He had forcefully kicked sugreev out of his Kingdom and had also snatched his wife and had made her one of his queens. Raam said according to dharma this was the most sinful act and the guilty must be punished. Raam then fought a battle with Bali and defeated him. He then gave the conquered kingdom back to Sugreev. When Bali was dying in the battlefield he mentioned to Raam about many good deeds he had done in his life. He then asked Raam the reason for him to support Sugreev . Raam replied, **"a younger brother's wife, a sister, a daughter-in-law and ones own daughter are alike."** Then he said whoever looks upon these with sinful eye must be punished. He further said that **stealing and/ or forcing other's wife to marry, is also a sinful act and the perpetrator must be severely punished**. Bali then succumbed to his injuries.

King, Sugreev's state flag had monkeys on its banner as emblem. Due to this reason, they were nicknamed as tribes of monkeys. Although, one of his ministers, Jambavant's tribe had bears on his banner as an emblem, they all, however, were collectively called the "Tribe of Monkeys." They all were of the opinion that wild life is very important for the ecological balance; therefore, they must be protected. This was a kind of, symbolically representing their collective dedication to the wild life protection.

Then Sugreev summoned the leaders and ministers of his "tribe of monkeys" and asked them to prepare a strategy to find Sita. He gave this responsibility to his ministers, Neel, Angad, Jambavant and Hanuman. Under the guidance of these people, who had a great knowledge of the area and its terrain and had wisdom and skills for such work, the task of finding Sita was initiated.

Hanuman Finds and Meets Sita & Vibhushan

With earlier information from Jatayu and later confirmatory evidences from others, it was now known that Raven had taken Sita to the Island of Lanka where his Capital was located. This Island Kingdom was very rich and therefore was nicknamed, "Golden Lanka." Among all other ministers of Sugreev, Hanuman had the most strength, endurance and skills to cross the straight. In addition, he also had previous contacts with local officials who could help him locate Sita in enemy territory. Therefore, it was decided that Hanuman would go and locate Sita and take Raam's message to her. In accordance with the plan, Hanuman crossed the strait and went to Lanka. He finally found out where Sita was being imprisoned. Finding an opportune time when all the prison guards were sleeping, Hanuman slipped into the compound and introduced him as Raam's messenger. As a proof he also presented Sita with Raam's special ring which Sita quickly recognized. Hanuman gave Sita, Raam's message that she should not get disappointed. Hanuman continued by saying that Raam would soon come, defeat the evil Ravan and bring her back with him. Sita then informed Hanuman that there are some good people in Ravan's court like Ravan's brother Vibhishan, who are honest, God fearing and believed in Dharm. Hanuman, then had a meeting with Vibhishan and asked him to tell Ravan that Raam had arrived on the other side of the shore and will soon cross the strait. He asked him to advise Ravan to release Sita and follow the path of Dharm. Hanuman then departed and came back with the message from Sita for Raam. The message was that she is well and was eagerly waiting for Raam to come and release her from Ravan's prison.

Vibhishan's Advice to Ravan Followed by His Expulsion by Ravan

Ravan's wife Mandoderi repeatedly tried to convince him to follow the path of Dharm and release Sita. Ravan would not heed. Then one of Ravan's prudent ministers named Malyavan unsuccessfully tried to change Ravan's mind; but he would not listen. Most of Ravan's advisors and ministers were anti-Dharm and believed in leading sinful life. Therefore they all supported him in not releasing Sita and in the policy of continually opposing Raam's path of Dharm. On other hand, Ravan's younger brother, though a pious and spiritual soul and disagreed with Ravan's way of life, earlier did not strongly oppose him. But now when Ravan had indulged in too many sinful acts, especially abducting other's wife and trying to marry her against her will, Vibhishan decided to strongly oppose him. Vibhishan said to his brother Ravan that in the heart of every man is found either wisdom or unwise judgment. By citing Vedas, Vibhishan said, "Where there is wisdom there is prosperity; where there is unwise judgment it leads to sinful behavior that ends in misfortune." He urged that Ravan , for the sake of his well being, should restore Sita to her husband. Ravan became very angry and expelled Vibhshan out of his kingdom. Vibhishan then went across the shore and joined Raam.

Raam and Ravan Fight and Ravan defeated

Raam then summoned his counselors and asked them to prepare for building a bridge so "that the army may pass over" it. Jambavant then asked help from two expert bridge builders for this project. These two brothers named Nal and Neel were clever building craftsmen specializing in bridge building. They chalked out the plan, established the most appropriate alignment and drafted strong people to haul and deploy rocks, mud and timber in specific manner. The morale among Raam's troops was so great that within a very short period of time the bridge was completed. As mentioned earlier, Raam's family was Vishu worshiper, and Raam himself was a worshiper of God of Vedas. On the other hand Ravan was Shiv worshiper so was Sita's father's family. Since Raam believed in the freedom of the way of worshiping and respected other's way of worship, he wanted to make it clear that he was not attacking Ravan because of him worshiping shiv. It was only because Ravan was not following the path of Dharma, was involved in sinful actions and was punishing and killing people who would not follow his way of worship. **Raam** therefore, first **worshiped Shiv** before ordering his army to cross the bridge and invade Ravan and get the release of imprisoned Sita. After worshiping shiv, the army marched towards Lanka. On reaching Lanka, Raam's army encamped on Mount Suvel.

Next day, Raam summoned his counselors and asked for their advice. Jambvant suggested and all agreed that **first Raam should try to have negotiations, on equal footing, and if all other peaceful ways have been exhausted then and only then Raam should invade, i.e., war should be the last resort**. Therefore, Ram sent Angad, Bali's son (Bali was Ravan's old friend), as an emissary for initiating a negotiated settlement. Ravan insulted Angad and asked him to go back to Raam with an angry massage that challenged Raam for a fight. After exhausting all reasonable alternatives Angad came back to Raam.

Finally, the fighting ensued. Ravan had a strong, well trained and experienced army under the direction of skilled generals like Meghnad and Kumbhkaran. Ravan, himself, was a great fighter. The fighting continued for many days. Many battles were won and lost by both sides. In one fierce battle, Laxman, was severely injured and was unconscious for many days and finally recovered with the timely use of herbal medicine. In the end, Ravan and his mighty generals were killed and his army surrendered. Raam ordered that all Ravan's surviving soldiers who were running away should not be chased because it was against Dharm to attack a person who has been defeated and is running away from the battle. **Raam also pardoned all surviving soldiers and urged them to respect other persons' ways of worship, serve the weak, poor and downtrodden, do not indulge in sinful acts and follow the path of Dharm.**

5.5 RAAM RETURNS TO AYODHYA AND HIS REIGN: "RAM RAJYA"

After Ravan's death, Vibhishan performed his funeral rites and gave him due respect as required by the tradition for an emperor and a learned person, which he was. Raam did not enter the capital city since he had promised to his father that he will work and live with forest and village dwellers only, for fourteen years. After performing Ravan's funeral rites Vibhishan went to meet Raam.

Vibhishan and His People Rule Lanka

Then Vibhishan returned to meet Raam. He and his people were very delighted and expressed their gratitude to Raam for liberating them from the sinful behavior of Ravan. Raam then asked King Sugreev, Hanuman and other ministers to accompany Vibhishan to the capital city and crown him the king. Raam then advised Vibhushan that he must not interfere in others' ways of worship. He however said that he and his citizens must follow the path of Dharm.

Raam then addressed his supporters and thanked them. He also said that with their dedication, faith in God and their promise to lead a sinless life made it possible to defeat such a powerful and resourceful but sinful Ravan.

Raam then sent Hanuman to inform Sita, who was imprisoned in a garden within the city boundary that they had defeated the evil forces and he had been sent by Raam to bring her out of the prison. In the meantime, Raam asked his followers to prepare for an *Ygny* ceremony. In this ceremony, a ceremonial fire is lit and all participants assemble around it to thank God of Vedas by chanting and singing the praise of God, the Almighty. When Sita arrived all bowed in respect for her and Raam greeted her with great love. They then performed the *Ygny* ceremony, gave thanks to God and then prepared to return to Ayyodhya after completing fourteen years of work among the people outside the cities.

Raam Returns to Ayodhya

Then Raam addressed the troops, his followers and leaders of various groups. He again thanked them, reminded them to follow the path of Dharm. He told them to return to their homes, **remember God, be faithful and fear no one**. They obediently followed Raam's instructions with mixed feeling of joy and sorrow and then went home to lead their pious lives. Then, Raam, Sita and Laxman rode on a fast traveling vehicle and started their journey back to Ayodhya. Some of his close associates, disciples and followers also accompanied Raam in his journey. On the way Raam also met all sages and many people he had helped to follow the righteous path. For a brief period he stayed with them and preached among them. They were very happy to see their friend, helper and teacher, after a long period of time, and were thankful to the Almighty who enabled Raam become successful in defeating the evil. Now they were completely convinced that God was with them through Raam. As Raam's vehicle approached Ayodhya and the good news of his arrival reached there, Bharat, raj guru (royal teacher), leaders of the society and the citizens flocked to celebrate his arrival. They painted their houses and lit the entire city with colorful lights. The homecoming of the Great Soul was celebrated with great enthusiasm and delight. This occasion is still celebrated throughout the Indian subcontinent as the festival of Diwali (the festival of lights) to commemorate the victory of good over the evil. Raam then took charge of his duties as the King of Koshal and emperor of the land.

Ram Reign : Establishes "Ram Rajya"

When Raam ascended the throne all rejoiced and "no one felt any enmity towards another." Every one was **"devoted to duty, the people trod the path of the Vedas, each according to their abilities, interest and stage of life, and enjoyed happiness, and lived without fear, or sorrow, or sickness"** (Uttarkand : 20). All citizens irrespective of their "way of worship" followed "Dharm" and were treated equal. All men and women loved one another. "Righteousness with its four pillars (viz., Truth, Purity, Compassion, and Charity) reigned throughout the land. There were healthcare services and there was no malnutrition. There was no premature death. Education was freely available to all. Raam's **"good governance by example"** resulted in the following attributes in his Kingdom (Raj):

1. **All men and women were good, pious and recognized the merits of others.**
2. **All citizens valued learning.**
3. **All men and women were generous and charitable.**
4. **Every husband was pledged to a vow of monogamy and each wife was devoted to her husband in thought and word and deed.**
5. **Wild lives and wilderness were protected.**
6. **Animal husbandry for agricultural and milk production purposes were encouraged resulting in abundance of milk and food products.**
7. **Mining and water resources prospered.**
8. **Everyone worshiped the Supreme Lord the way they realized the God and all followed the path of Dharm.**

Overall, there was happiness and prosperity in Raam's reign. That is why, even today after many thousands of years, people long for coming of an ideal reign like Raam's and an ideal ruler similar to Raam. "Raam Rajya" is every person's dream. All the faithful therefore, believe Raam to have a "Godly Character and God like Soul." Raam reigned for a long period of time and after his death his successors followed the basic principals of good rule established by him.

5.6: OVERVIEW AND RAAM'S GIFT TO HUMANITY

Prior to Raam's birth, Indian philosophy, theology and culture had evolved over many thousands of years. In general, everybody living in the subcontinent followed the same Dharm but had numerous Ways of Worship, each to his or her interest, liking and/or bringing up.

Dharm means duty: In general, the Dharm of every Indian (here I mean the person living in the Indian subcontinent) was to follow the following main tenets:

- Honor thy father, mother, guru (teacher) and elders.
- Have mutual love, respect and trust between you and your spouse and both men and women must be monogamous.
- Engage in actions that will lead to the betterment of the weak and the poor.
- Get away from *Kam* (lust), *Krodh* (anger), *Lobh* (greed), *Moh* (wordly attachment), *Muthe* (intoxication), and *Matsarya* (jealousy).
- Love, value and protect human life.
- Respect all ways of worship to God.

Thus Dharm was a kind of "the Law of the Land".

 Freedom for the Ways of Worship: All ways of worship to God are to be respected and valued. The theology had evolved to the level that it was generally accepted that various paths can lead to the Kingdom of God.

Thus, every Indian had to follow the same Dharm but at the same time could have different ways of worship; this is a kind of separation of "church and the state"

At the time Raam was born, cracks had already developed in the society based on the theology and the social status of individuals. Although the land was rich and fertile, generally masses were well off and were being ruled by their own people, **great divides between the people** based on their **ways of worship and social status** were quite evident throughout the land. A major class divide had also developed between the rulers and the ruled as well as between the city and town dwellers and the forest (wood) dwellers. There were many social and political leaders who were **not following what they were preaching**.

There was a great debate across the land and in the entire society about the supremacy and even the truthfulness and the existence of ones way of worship to the God. Although various denominations propagated that their form of God was omnipotent and omnipresent, Vishnu and Shiv followers believed that the God only can take the form of their definition of God. The God of Vedic Traditions, however, in addition to being compassionate, omnipotent and omnipresent was also indivisible, infinite and invisible. These different denominations now instead of respecting each others way of worship would many times insult others' ways of worship. Most of these denominations were generally vocal about expressing the superiority of their ways of worship but would not use force to convince others to follow their way of worship.

On the contrary, a large and powerful group of people, called Rakshash, were forcibly imposing their way of worship on others and openly disregarding the principles of Dharm. In leading this life style, they would harm others, steal and acquire forcefully what was others' and openly went against the ways of Dharm. Their sinful acts would cause major pain and suffering among the common masses, especially those in the weaker sections of the population.

In the city of Ayodhya, capital of the Kingdom of Koshal, situated on the banks of River Saryu, in the Indo-Gangatic valley, a king named Dashrath reigned. He was renowned, powerful, righteous and wise. He was a sincere devotee of Vishnu but he respected all other ways of worship. In his old age, with God's blessings, he had four sons: Raam, Bharat, Laxman and Shatrughan.

As the brothers grew up, in accordance with the tradition, they were sent to their guru's educational institution. Raam learnt all the disciplines of education including theology and the art of using arms. He "became proficient in scholarship and modesty and virtue and decorum and practiced all princely sports." With time, Raam became an expert archer, and mastered war techniques. He also became well versed in Vedas, theology, administration and philosophy.

A sage named Vishwamitra (meaning a friend of the entire world) lived in his Ashram in the forest where he practiced yoga (yoge), practiced meditation, preached to who ever came to hear him and worshiped the God of Vedas (indivisible and invisible one God). There were some people with Satanic and Devilish philosophy, who did not like this way of worship and philosophy. They would destroy Vishwamitra's places of worship and attack his followers. Sage Vishwamitra came to king Dashrath and asked him to send Raam and his brother Laxman to protect his Ashram.

Raam and Laxman , following the path of Dharm, accompanied the sage to his Ashram. There they further learnt the theology of Vedas and about God. They also learnt survival techniques and obtained the knowledge about various herbs and their medicinal powers. As they lived in the Ashram, away from the luxuries of the urban living, they also learnt about the ways many people in the kingdom lived. They had to engage in many battles to protect the sage and his followers. In the end, they were successful in their mission and defeated the evil forces. Since this was the first time, after completing his education in his guru's institute, that Raam by himself fought wars to protect righteous people, it was a sort of apprenticeship for him. In this mission he **protected the weak and fought to keep the freedom of worship for others**. This was a selfless and holy mission of Dharm.

One day, sage Vishwamitra took Raam to participate in the "ceremony of the contest of the bow" in Janakpuri. On the way they saw a lonely hermitage. The hermitage belonged to sage Gautam, who unfairly blamed his wife, Ahilya, for having sex with another man. Because of this the entire community broke relationships with her. Now, Ahilya would spend her time in praying and serving the out casts. When Raam heard this story his heart was filled with compassion. He went to meet Ahilya, praised her for her service to God. When, people saw that a great sage like Vishwamitra and a soul like Raam have given honor to Ahilya they all repented for their sins. Raam preached to all to **give respect to women and treat them as equals. People then gave up all entanglements of deceit**.

Then Raam went to Janakpuri, met Sita, both fell in love with one another, won the contest and married Sita. Raam's family was worshiper of Vishnu while Sita's was worshiper of Shiv. Therefore, Shiv followers objected to this marriage. A great debate ensued about the freedom of worship. After a long and heated debate, Raam convinced the assembly that it was sinful to force one's way of worship on others. He stressed that all must have the right to follow their way of worship.

After returning home with his bride, Raam began helping his father in running the administration. He was so efficient, just and compassionate administrator that with the advice of all ministers and raj guru (royal teacher), the king decided to invest Raam with regal powers. Hearing this news, all citizens were delighted. However, the wise men and the sages of the land realized that a person like Raam was needed to protect the week and the poor and to preach among the ignorant. They prayed to God to help them. God then commanded king's favorite queen to convince him to send Raam to the forests in the service of humanity for fourteen years. Even though, Raam knew that he will have to lead a very difficult life full of many dangers, for the sake of week and poor and to protect Dharm he gladly accepted the mission; this he knew was a way to serve God. He accompanied by his wife and brother, Laxaman, proceeded to live amongst and serve the disadvantaged.

On his way, Raam met many sages, forest dwellers and various tribes. He discussed theology with the sages and promised them protection to worship and meditate with freedom. He met and lived with forest dwellers and various tribes and asked them to be free from their sins. **He also preached them to be proud of their profession, heritage and the way of their worship and urged them to follow the path of Dharm**. Raam's key message was that the simplest **way to the Kingdom of God is through:**

- **Devotion (Bhakti)**
- **Leading a sinless life (Nishpap)**
- **Service (doing good to others), and**
- **Follow the path of Dharm**

Evil people did not like Raam's mission. They caused many obstructions and even forcefully abducted Sita in his absence. Raam with the help of his disciples of various backgrounds: city dwellers, villagers, forest dwellers and chiefs and commoners alike, defeated the sinners and evil forces. After fourteen years of service to the humanity, Raam returned to Ayodhya with Sita and Laxamn. He then ascended the throne and ruled as an ideal king for a long time.

Raam's "**good governance by example**" resulted in the following attributes in his Kingdom (Raj):

1. **All men and women were good, pious and recognized the merits of others.**
2. **All citizens valued learning.**
3. **All men and women were generous and charitable.**
4. **Every husband was pledged to a vow of monogamy and each wife was devoted to her husband in thought and word and deed.**
5. **Wild lives and wilderness were protected.**
6. **Animal husbandry for agricultural and milk production purposes were encouraged resulting in abundance of milk and food products.**
7. **Mining and water resources prospered.**
8. **Everyone worshiped the Supreme Lord the way they realized the God and all followed the path of Dharm.**

Dharm means duty: In general, the path of Dharm means to follow the following main tenets:

- **Honor thy father, mother, guru (teacher) and elders.**
- **Have mutual love, respect and trust between you and your spouse and both men and women must be monogamous.**
- **Engage in actions that will lead to the betterment of the weak and the poor.**
- **Get away from *Kam* (lust), *Krodh* (anger), *Lobh* (greed), *Moh* (wordly attachment), *Muthe* (intoxication), and *Matsarya* (jealousy).**
- **Love, value and protect human life.**
- **Respect all ways of worship to God.**

Overall, there was happiness and prosperity in Raam's reign. That is why, even today after many thousands of years, people of Indian subcontinent origin and those who are proud of their origin, long for coming of an ideal reign like Raam's and an ideal ruler like Raam. "Raam Rajya" is every ones dream. All the faithful therefore, believe Raam to have a "Godly Character and God like Soul."

6

BUDH

6.1 INDIAN SUBCONTINENT PRIOR TO AND AT THE TIME OF BUDH'S BIRTH

As discussed previously, in the Indian subcontinent there was a distinction between the way of worship (religion) and the Dharm, which is the way of leading ones life in a society i.e., following certain Laws. Thus, theology (the systematic study of God and His divinity) could be openly discussed and people could agree or disagree with one another on the matter of their way of worship without the fear of being penalized as long as they followed Dharm; the main tenets of Dharm have been presented in the previous chapter on Raam. In other words, as long as people followed Dharm, there was complete freedom on the way of worship. Due to this reason the theology evolved with time and in many cases the new theological principles or doctrines incorporated in them many of the previously acquired tenets. Thus evolution and accumulation of ideas and experiences on divinity continued.

Evolution & Accumulation of Theology in Indian Subcontinent Prior to the Period of Budh's Birth

The earliest theological philosophy of the people residing in Indian subcontinent, during the period many thousands years before Budh, who was born in the year 563 B.C., was recorded in **Vedic scriptures**. This philosophy recognized the Almighty as the supreme power but also personified various powers, such as, fire, sun and wind as gods who actually were described as having divine powers. For example, Indr is described to have astounding valor and Varun is described to be the upholder of moral and physical order in the world. According to Vedic theology, a righteous person would go to dwell in heaven. Rituals were simple ceremonies in front of an altar consisting of a single fire. The fire was a kind of witness, to evoke God, on significant occasions, such as, birth, marriage or a special celebration to Thank God. As sages and learned people pondered and meditated about the way(s) of attaining liberation from worldly bondage, they began to contemplate about the following questions (Ch'en, 1968):

- Is there a unity behind the universe?
- Is there one absolute truth behind all the phenomena around us?
- If there is unity, what is the nature of it?
- What is the relation of this Absolute to the individual self?

As seers and sages contemplated and meditated they further realized the omnipotence, omnipresence and oneness (Monotheistic) nature of God. This was recorded in the scriptures called **Upnishads**. Upnishads expound that behind the diversities of the world there is one universal unity, the supreme Brahm. People may call it or worship it in different forms, e.g., Vishnu, Shiv, or other forms, but they all are one and the same. As Ch'en,(1968), says **"Upnishads see Brahm in everything, and everything in Brahm."** Brahm is considered to pervade the whole universe and thus is a cosmic power.

Concurrently, quest for the relationship between the cosmic and psychic (the inner self or Atman) powers was going on amongst the seers. This quest led to the belief that the "inner self" is a pure consciousness. It was further realized by some of these seers that pure consciousness (the true self), freed from all bodily and mental limitations "was realized through self-intuition, a mystical state that transcended wakefulness, sleep, and dream. When a man realized his true self in the mystical state, his only experience was that of pure bliss." After discovering the inner essence of a man, the seers of Upnishads propounded, that Brahm, the inner essence of the universe is the same as Atman. This led to the further belief that after going through a long process of training, meditation and good deeds one can become enlightened and can experience that unity in ones own experience. Finally, after realizing the "great truth" through this process one is said to have attained liberation or release from the cycle of rebirth. Thus, the Indian seers enunciated "the truth that the Supreme Being which is the universal cause and source of all existence is also the inner ruler of man" (Ch'en, 1968).

At the same time, many other theologies were being expounded, taught and discussed by other sages who belonged to various independent schools of theologies that existed throughout the land. There were also many people, who would wander about either alone or in groups and would engage in debates with one another, and engage in teaching their ways of achieving enlightenment. In accordance with the tenets of Dharm, all these ways, even if they may be different from ones belief, were respected by the population. Since these ascetics were the men who took similar vows, such as, non-violence, engaged in the search for truth, avoided theft, sexual continence, and renunciation of property, chastity and poverty, people respected them and gave them food and shelter even though they may not agree with some of their teachings. Such was, in general, the theological environment of the Indian subcontinent prior to the birth of Budh.

Theological, Social and Political Environments in Indian Sucontinent During the Fifth & Sixth Century B.C.

Theological Environment:

In the fifth and sixth century B.C., a majority of the population, in the Indian subcontinent, followed the **Vedic Tradition**. They believed in doing good deeds and worshiping the omnipotent and omnipresent one God. However, with time some of the priests began making the worship rituals very complicated and began stressing too much on these rituals as a means of human salvation. As in the past, other ways of worships enjoyed full freedom. Similarly, ascetics continued their search for enlightenment in their own way. In addition to this, there were other theological teachers who were propagating their way of interpretations of the creation and its actions and reactions. Ch'en (1968) and Gour (1929) provide scholarly details on some or all of these theological ideas. Some of these were as follows:

- **Materialism**: Propagators of this philosophy believed that when a person dies, he returns to the four elements (earth, fire, water and air) of which we are made of. This meant good deeds would not yield to salvation. They did not believe in rebirth and thus felt that one should fully enjoy material things in this life.
- **Fortuitous Origin**: The teachers of this philosophy believed that whatever good or evil one did had no effect on the individual.
- **Jains**: These teachers believed that one could alter the effects of past deeds by deliberate acts, especially austerities. The Jains therefore, emphasized restraint of senses, freedom from passions, penance and confession.
- **Rationalistic Sankhya Philosophy**: This philosophy's main teacher was Kapil. According to this belief there is no God or Supreme creator. Their teacher would say that a benevolent God would not tolerate the misery, pain, cruelty, injustices, decay and death. Kapil postulated the existence of matter and the soul. According to Kapil the soul remains only a passive spectator. Matter is unconscious but contains in itself the power of evolution while *Karm* (action) alone determines the course of that evolution.

Although, Vedantic Tradition believed in God and Sankhyic philosophy did not, they both appear to have agreed on the practice of meditative Yoge as enlarging the vision beyond the material horizon (Gour, 1929).

Political Environment:

During the fifth and sixth century B.C., around one thousand five hundred years after Raam, the subcontinent was now divided into many kingdoms and a number of republics. The most powerful kingdoms in the north were the kingdoms of Koshal (later Oudh and presently the province of Uttar Pradesh) and Magadh (presently the province of Bihar). The kingdom of Magadh, located in the eastern portion of the Ganges Valley, was ruled by a king named Bimbeshwar. North of Magadh was Koshal and was ruled by king Prasannajit.

The republics were governed by a council of notables or supreme assembly, presided by an elected President (*Nayak*) who held office for a number of years. "The assembly was a popular body whose proceedings were regulated by definite rules concerning the passing of resolutions, the constitution of a quorum, and the establishment of committees to transact business." One such republic in this area was in Brij (now the Muzaffarnagar district in the province of Bihar) with its capital in Vaisali. Budh, later, organized his monastic community after the pattern of these republican assemblies (Ch'en, 1968).

Overall, the land was relatively at peace and free from internal strives and foreign invaders.

Social Environment:

Unlike in the previous periods when a person's occupation decided his class and social status, now different guilds wanted to protect their trade secrets and thus the society was generally divided into casts based on their birth. The four casts or groups were Brahman (priest and intellectual), Kshatriy (warrior), Vaishy (merchant), and Shudra (laborer). There was no free social mobility as was common in the past. Brahmans held the dominant position in the society. All this caused a major resentment among many theological, social and political thinkers.

The village was an important administrative unit in a kingdom and a republic. The village, in the either governing system, was administered by the village *Panchayat* or council of elders. Population, irrespective of their way of worship and theological belief, in general, followed the tenets of Dharm. The economy was primarily agriculture based. However, trade and animal husbandry were also important for the economy and the society. The population, in general, was well fed from the standards of sixth century B. C. There was a large economic middle class; this resulted in producing a large number of social, political and theological thinkers. There was no slavery but there were many landless people who would do hard labor for wages; food and shelter could be obtained relatively easily. The family ties were strong and a person followed family traditions faithfully; this included marriage, business and other social traditions.

It was under such theological, political and social environment that Gautam Budh was born in the year 563 B.C.

6.2 BUDH'S BIRTH, MARRIAGE AND RENUNCIATION

Budh's Parents, Birth and Early Education

Sudhodhan, Gautam Budh's father, was a chieftain of a small state of Kapilvastu, which was located in the current province of Uttar Pradesh. Kapilvastu was situated to the north of Benares (**Figure 6.1**). The counrty side of the area consists of rolling plains and has rich soil washed from the Himlayan outskirts to the north. The land produces rice and has a variety of trees, such as, tall Sal trees, ever-green Mango fruit trees and the large and shade provider Peepal trees. The climate of the area is cold in winter (October to March), extremely hot in summer (March to June) and monsoon rains from June to October. Sudhodhan belonged to Shakya clan, was a small chieftain and thus ruled an area of about fifty miles by about forty miles. Sudhodhan had a ruling alliance with the King of Koshal.

Sudhodhan had two wives named Mahamaya and Mahapajapati. When Mahamaya, the elder queen, became pregnant she had a dream of the entry of a white elephant in her womb. The king sent for the dream interpreters. Their interpretation was that "a son will be born unto thee,----. When he forsakes love, royal power and palace,-----, wanders forth in pity for the whole world, he will become Budh, to be honored by the three worlds and he will make glad the universe with the marvelous nectar of immortality"(Lalit Vistar 22-23 as cited by Gaur,1929). When queen Mahamaya was traveling from the capital city Kapilvastu to her parents' place to have her first child, she gave birth to her son on the way under a large Sal tree in the Lumbini village grove. The child was named Sidharth Gautam(Gautam being his family name). He was born on the full moon day of the month of Vesakh (April-May) in 563 B.C. It is recorded that many miracles took place to exhibit that this was the birth of a being destined to attain perfect Enlightenment. An old sage, named Asit, on visiting the palace predicted that the child "had come to the earth to teach suffering humanity how to eradicate misery." The birth of the child was rejoiced by all in the town.

Just seven days after Sidharth's birth his mother died and he was then raised by his step mother. When the child became of school age he "was put to school under the tutelage of Vishwamitr." He was taught language, arithmetic and Veds. **As the prince grew older he preferred solitude and meditation** instead of games and other activities which young adults of his age would normally get involved

Marriage

Sidharth's father noticed his son's unusual inclinations and decided to have him married to break his habits and bring his interests back to the traditional behavior of a young prince. Several eligible maidens were found and Sidharth was asked to marry one he liked. Initially, Sidharth did not agree to marry. After some time he finally agreed to marry Gopi, the daughter of Dandapani belonging to Shakya clan. Dandapani objected marrying his daughter to a person who had never shown proficiency and skills in traditional learning and sports. When confronted by his own father about this issue, prince Sidharth agreed to exhibit his skills in the presence of an assembly in seven days. On the appointed day, "there were five hundred Shakya youths against whom Gautam successfully completed in calligraphy, arithmetic, archery and wrestling." This satisfied all including Dandapani, king Sudhodhan and Gopi. Thus, Sidharth and Gopi were married after Sidharth successfully exhibited his proficiency in the skills.

After marriage, Sidharth's inclinations towards solitude, asceticism and meditation were overpowered by his attraction to his beautiful bride Gopi (also named as princess Yasodhara) and he now agreed to enter in the activities of ordinary household affairs. During the years following marriage, Sidharth spent his time in regal splendor in three different palaces built to adapt three seasons of the year. He was surrounded by women attendants who played music and various entertaining dances for him. For a while,

Figure 6.1 The Geographical Area Where Budh Was Born
(Base Map: Courtesy of The General Libraries UT at Austin, 2003)

it appeared that he was enjoying all these pleasures of life. The union of Sidharth and Yasodhara also resulted in the birth of their son, Rahul.

Renunciation

Although Sidharth now had every worldly thing at his disposal and had a happy family life, he began feeling as if something was still missing spiritually. He periodically began yearning for change. His inner thought awakened him and one day he came out of his luxurious palace garden and went outside. While on his way outside the palace and in deep thoughts, he had his **first encounter with misery**; until then he was shielded from the miseries of the world.

(One should realize that we all see such miseries all the time but do not notice them the way Sidharth did.)

- He saw **an old man** on the road. The man was worn out, had broken teeth, grey hair, bent body, uttering inarticulate sounds and was walking with a cane that too with great difficulty. Seeing this Sidharth asked his charioteer, "What human form is this, so miserable and so distressing, the like of which I have never seen before?" The charioteer simply replied that it "is called an old man." Sidharth then asked about the meaning of "old." The charioteer responded by saying that old meant the decay of the body and its vital functions and also the loss of memory and the decay of the mental faculties. When asked by Sidharth if that was a universal law, his charioteer responded by saying, "Yes." He further added that the **universal law is, "all that is born must die."**

- On a second occasion Sidharth saw a **sick man** on the road. The man had high fever, his body was exhausted, had difficulty in breathing and he was without shelter. After enquiring about this state of a fellow human being, his charioteer told him that, "**such sickness is common to all.**"

- On a third instance, Sidharth saw **a dead man being carried away** for cremation and was surrounded by his weeping and lamenting friends and relatives. Discussions ensued between the charioteer and Sidharth and in the end it was concluded that a dead body was like a fallen tree and his loved ones (father, mother, wife, children and friends) will see him no more and **in the end we all must come to this fate**.

- On the fourth occasion, Sidharth saw **an ascetic monk** who appeared tranquil and full of self-control. His every action, such as, bending, stretching, wearing of his coat, eating, etc, all **exhibited peace of mind**. The charioteer mentioned that the man had forsaken his family, friends and relatives; he had devoted himself to charity and had controlled his desires. He added that the man would not hurt any one and would do good to all.

All this fired Sidharth's imagination and he wanted to renounce the world immediately and he wished to learn how to selflessly do good to humanity. Attachment to his infant baby, his wife and his father still were strong for Sidharth and he could not leave his home immediately. However, the more he contemplated about the miseries of the world the more he wanted to seek a way that would lead to human salvation from its sufferings and the miseries. Finally, Prince Sidharth Gautam decided to become ascetic Gautam at the age of twenty nine. He had his hair and beard shaved, put on yellow garments, left his home, family and friends, renounced all luxuries of life and became an ascetic.

The following is a chronology of Sidharth from his birth to his renunciation:

- King **Sudhodhan** had a son named **Sidharth** Gautam
- Prince Sidharth married **Gopi** (princess Yasodhara)
- Sidharth and Yasodhara had a son named **Rahul**
- On renunciation and after achieving enlightenment Sidharth was called **Gautam Budh**

6.3 ACHIEVING ENLIGHTENMENT

Seven Years of Preparation

For the first six years of his renunciation and in search of truth, Sidharth visited various spiritual teachers and institutions of the time and learnt the theological principles and meditative techniques from them. He also discussed personally the rival doctrines with their exponents. **First he visited the teachers of Orthodox school** who believed that the liberation can only be secured by offering the sacrifice and subjecting the body to mortification. He quickly rejected this doctrine. **Then he visited the renowned teacher, Arad Kalap, of Sankhya philosophy.** He was reputed to have enjoined poverty and the subjugation of senses (as different from self-torture) and the practice of Yoge. Sidharth settled down as a disciple of Arad and in due course mastered his doctrine. Sidharth was seeking a way that would lead him to the liberation of soul from the cycle of births and death. He did not find the answer to this question in Sankhya philosophy. He therefore left his tutor, Arad, and left for Magadh, an area around Kasi or Banares, a city reputed for its centers of learning. Then he went to Rajgrah kingdom to meet another teacher named Rudrak. Rudrak was a philosophical Nihilist that did not satisfy Sidharth. After this Sidharth went to the neighboring town of Gaya and fixed his lonely habitation on the bank of the River Niranjan. Although Sidharth, by this time had learned and experienced different systems of philosophies and his mind was more calm and peaceful, still at the deepest level of his unconscious mind he felt that his mind was not totally pure.

At this time, Sidharth decided to practice self-mortification by practicing rigorous austerities (by fasting and other acts of self-denial) with five other seekers of salvation. As a result he was reduced to mere skeleton, "yet real wisdom still eluded him." With this experience Sidharth realized that either of the two extremes (i) a life led with all physical luxuries or (ii) a life led with physical torture and sever penance would not lead to Enlightenment. **"This realization turned him towards a middle path."** He then started taking food and decided to stay away from rigorous austerities. His five companions, who still believed that self-mortification was the way to Enlightenment, left him. He decided to continue his search alone.

Sidharth then, on a full moon day in the month of Vasakh (April-May), after taking a refreshing bath in the Niranjan River and then drinking milk, sat down below the shade of a Pipal tree. He sat there with the determination that he would not leave his seat till he attained Enlightenment. "He spent that night in deep meditation and rediscovered the long-lost technique of Vipassan." **During this meditation, Mar, the Demon, tried to tempt him** with Confusion, Gaiety, Pride, Lust, Delight and Thirst. After he failed in his seduction technique, the demon tried intimidation and coercion. Sidharth repulsed all these successfully. Then he experienced the ultimate truth in all its purity. "He penetrated the illusion of a solid mind and body, dissolved the tendency of his mind to cling and crave, and realized the unconditioned truth." Sidharth Gautam became Gautam Budh (The wise, The Enlightened), the tree under which he sat became known as Bodhi tree and the area became known as Bodhgaya.

During this meditative state Bhudh with his pure and divine sight saw the **universal truth** as follows:
- **He saw that the living beings under the influence of evil actions pass through wretched worlds and those with good actions go toward in heaven.**
- **He then reflected that men's minds were ruled by desire. Desire arises where there is sensation, and sensation is produced by contact.**
- **Contact arises through six organs of the senses. These arise in the organism, where there is incipient consciousness, which arises from later impressions left by former actions, which again arise from ignorance.**
- **Thus ignorance is the root of the great trunk of pain. Therefore, ignorance is to be stopped by those who seek liberation.**

This was Budh's Enlightenment. This gave him the grip of the real cause of human sorrow, and the middle path was the suggested remedy. Then Budh sat for seven days under the Bodhi tree in meditation and enjoyed the bliss of Enlightenment. He then meditated under a banyan tree for seven days. It is here, to a question, "Who is a true Brahmin (the one who knows Brahm)?" he responded that a **true Brahmin is "one free from evil and pride, self-restrained, learned and pure**." Then he meditated under another tree for seven days and heavy storm was raised to distract his thought during this meditation; this also he conquered. Thus he had meditated by performing four "*Dhyans*" or meditations that symbolize "the four stages of progress in the path to knowledge." In Indian traditional meditations, these *Dhyans* are the *Yoge* (joining of the human soul with the Divine).

Bhudh had thus spent seven years in achieving Enlightenment. He was now thirty six years old.

Budh's Dilemma : Keep the Knowledge to Yourself or Share With Others

During the seven years of preparation and then during its last four weeks' of deep meditation, Budh had discovered the true path. He now began pondering if he should keep it to himself and enjoy the bliss by himself or if he should share it with others too. He was confident that he had penetrated the doctrine which was profound but difficult to understand especially by those who are intent upon desire. He also felt that explaining such difficult concepts of the law of causality and the chain of causation will be difficult subject and it will also be difficult for them to understand; this Budh felt would cause weariness and pain to him. His main concern was that what he had acquired with great pain will be discarded by people who are lost in lust and hatred.

As Budh pondered more about the difficult task of explaining the doctrine to others, he was tempted to enjoy the Bliss by himself and not to preach the doctrine to others. When Budh was pondering about this dilemma, the devil Mar's (Satan's) wicked voice was heard by him; the wicked voice of devil Mar advised him to enter in Nirvan (without desire or the state of eternal bliss) by himself and not to worry about other people's salvation. Budh then replied to Mar, "O wicked one, I shall not enter Nirvan, until I" have gathered, trained and prepared my disciples and have successfully ordained monks and nuns who will then propagate the doctrine among all mankind.

Budh Ordains First Five Disciples

With the clear vision and determination in his mind Budh decided to disseminate his views and enlist disciples. His first thought was to go to his first teachers to whom he had gone to learn and who he felt could understand the truth he had realized; but both of them were dead by that time. Then his thoughts turned to his first disciples who had deserted him because they wanted to pursue the path of self-mortification to achieve The Enlightenment. These five Bhikshus (a beggar who begs instructions for mind) were now seeking the path to Eternal Truth in the Holy city of Benares. So he departed to the Holy City of Benares. When he came to the River Ganges he asked the ferryman to take him across the river; the ferryman asked for the toll fee. To this Budh replied that he had nothing and carried no material possession. Then Budh "flew across through the sky like the king of birds." On reaching Benares, Budh went to the Deer park Isipatan (now called Sarnath). After meeting these five Bhikshus, Budh told them that he had penetrated the truth and had achieved The Enlightenment. He said that he would teach them the path to Eternal Truth. In the beginning the five Bhikshus did not believe Budh but after a few discussions between them and spiritual discourses by Budh they were convinced that Budh was the Enlightened one and now they gave their full attention to what Budh had to say.

Budh then continued by saying that a life given to pleasure and lust is degrading as they already knew. On the other hand a life given to self-mortification, as they were following, is painful and dishonorable. He then said that by avoiding these two extremes and following the Middle Path he had gained the knowledge to Nirvan.

Then, Budh preached to his first five disciples in the following manner. He said that:

(A) The **noble truth of suffering** consists of (i) suffering in the birth, (ii) suffering in illness, (ii) suffering in decay, (iii) suffering in the object we dislike, (iv) suffering due to separation from our loved ones or things we love, and (v) suffering in the death. Thus, suffering is in clinging to these five existences.

(B) The **noble truth of the cessation of suffering** is complete abandoning every passion and desire.

(C) Finally, **Nirvan is achieved by following eight-fold path** that consists of: (i) Right Belief, (ii) Right Aspiration, (iii) Right Conduct, (iv) Right Speech, (v) Right Means of Livelihood, (vi) Right Memory, (vii) Right Endeavor, and (viii) Right Meditation.

After hearing this, the five Bhikshus were delighted and requested to be admitted in Bhudh's order which was duly accepted. Thus, these five were his first disciples and the first members of his order.

Budh Sends Missionaries in All Directions and Performs Miracles

As Bhudh preached his message, the number of his disciples grew fast. His message to his disciples was to travel from place to place for the welfare of the masses. He directed them **to preach the law, in spirit and in letter, so that people all over, irrespective of their background, become free from their bondage and achieve Eternal Bliss.** For example, he converted, to his doctrine, numerous priests, businessmen, and even robbers and harlots. The doors of his church were open to all, as long as they wanted to change and better their lives.

Budh trained, ordained and then sent his disciples in all directions to preach and make more converts. His pleasing personality and his persuasive speech was enthusiastically welcomed by his audience and they thronged in large numbers to hear him so that they could achieve happiness. People readily accepted his eight-fold path for achieving perfection. **His converts were from all casts, classes and occupations.** He told them "**Do not ask about descent, but ask about conduct.**"

As he preached and converted he **performed many miracles**. For example, he offered wealth to those who needed it. Budh cured the lame, insane and blind. He also healed sick people with various illnesses.

When he was asked by wealthy people, "**What was the use of riches**?" He replied, "**Charity**." When he was asked about cast, he said that **cast was occupational** as it had originally been; it has nothing to do with the birth of a person. For example, he said that whoever lives amongst men lives by cow-keeping is a husbandman, whoever amongst men lives by trade is a merchant and whoever amongst men lives by serving is a servant. Similarly, a man who is learned, a hero, a great sage, wise, has attained the highest good and is enlightened is a Brahmin.

He sent his disciples with these messages in all directions to spread his message for the welfare of humanity.

6.4 TWELVE YEARS OF PREACHING AND CONVERTING

Since time immemorial, in the Indian subcontinent most of the business had been carried out during the dry months that begin in October and end in June, about an eight-month period. During the remaining four monsoon months the roads and major travel routs become difficult to traverse. Therefore distance travels were limited during the dry - months of the year. In light of this, Budh's missionary work, therefore, followed the logistic that (1) the monks would travel places and preach during the dry eight months and (2) they would settle down in camps for planning and training purposes during the four monsoon rainy months. The monks would discuss their experiences and present plans for remainder of the year in these camps.

Budh normally would spend his time in these camps preaching to the worshipers who would throng to these camps. He would also train monks for their work. Generally, these camps will be located at delightful quiet places outside the towns and villages and will be on a mountain top or on a river bank. In this way, Budh spent twelve years of his ministry in preaching and converting.

Once on his way to Rajgrah, the capital city of the kingdom of Magadh, Budh stopped at Gaya. In Gaya a wealthy, influential orthodox Brahmin lived. He had a thousand pupils trained in vedic rites. This head-priest's family name was Kashyap. Budh discussed with him theology and tried to convince him by reason. But the head-priest would not get convinced with Budh's theological arguments. In the end, **Budh resorted to a shower of miracles** which finally impressed Kashyap of Budh's power. Eventually he along with his disciples and relatives accepted Budh's church. "Henceforward Budh's progression from village to village was a triumphal march and converts came to him, not in hundreds, but in thousands" (Gour, 1929). Budh then gained a strong following in the holy city of Benares and Gaya.

On reaching Rajgrah, Budh converted King Bimbeshwar and his employees to his theology. King's example was then followed by his numerous notables and subjects.

It was not that only the kings, the nobles, the Brahmins and law abiding citizens but also the social deviants, such as, robbers were also impressed by Budh's piety. Once as he was traveling and preaching he fell upon a nest of five hundred robbers. On meeting them he preached them and urged them to follow the righteous path. "They were all reclaimed and converted, and exchanged their tools of burglary for the bowls and staves of piety" (Mahavagga, XVII, as cited by Gour, 1929)

Budh's preaching generally followed a phased approach. He would first talk about the unrighteousness, corruption, vanity and the impurity of desires. Then he would present the glory of being free from desires. Finally, he would preach to his listeners on the origin of suffering and the way to be free from them. He would then say that their lives will be clean like a clean garment from which all impurities are removed. People liked all his presentations and his examples. Above all, they liked that he sacrificed all his luxuries for their sake and were very happy that he cared for human welfare.

Budh spent first rainy season in retreat at Sarnath with *Sangha*, which had grown to sixty *Arhant Bhikshus* (liberated monks). He spent his second, third and fourth rainy season camps in the Bamboo grove at Rajgrah. The fifth rainy season was spent at Vesali; this was the year when The *Bhikshuni Sangh* (**The Order of Nuns**) was established. The sixth and the seventh rainy season retreats were spent at Mankulapabbat and Tavatims, respectively. His eighth through twelfth retreats were organized at various other delightful locations where he planned, taught and prepared Bikshus for preaching.

In this way Budh spent twelve years preaching, converting and spreading the Gospel. He became well known across the land especially in the Kingdoms of Koshal and Magadh. By now, back in Kapilvastu, Budh's son had gotten married and had a daughter. His son persuaded his grandfather to send an invitation to Budh to come to their kingdom and preach. He accepted the invitation. On his way, he visited the fig tree under which he was born. He met his wife, step-mother, his son and grand daughter and other relatives. He was greeted with great love and affection by his clansmen. He converted several women headed by his own wife; they were then admitted in his Order. He then went to the capital city Kapilvastu where he met his father. His father and his son Rahul also joined his Order along with other members of the family.

6.5 ESTABLISHING AND CONSOLIDATING HIS CHURCH AND BUDH'S LAST DAYS

After meeting his family and converting many of his clansmen, admitting his wife, son and others in his Order, Budh returned from Kapilvastu and eventually settled down "to the practice of routine". As mentioned earlier, this routine was developed and established during his first twelve years of ministry. Budh's activities were primarily administered from three important centers, which were: Benares, Rajgrah and Savitthi. Unlike other smaller temporary and permanent locations, each of these three nerve centers of his ministry had large monasteries that had large lecture halls for monks, clergy and the lay people. Budh himself would travel to different places including to these centers in a well planned manner. Budh never made a permanent home in any of his centers; he always treated them as his camps. He always walked on foot and would not accept a conveyance or a pony like his fellow monks. **Thus he avoided attachment and exhibited no preferential treatment with a place or a group of people or monks.**

When Budh visited a town, his advanced party of monks would make all arrangements including letting the town's people know about the time and place of the program. All leading citizens and common folks would be invited to listen to the Master or The Blessed One, as he was called by then. Budh's teaching and preaching sessions were well planned and organized. Budh first would talk about the basic issues of life and death which everybody knew, and then he would bring up individual and society's short-comings and finally **he would offer his well tried and practical solutions.** For most people, in attendance, this was enough and they would, if they agreed with his discourse, convert to his faith. Then there was time allotted for those who wanted to have one-on-one discussions with The Blessed One. **Budh was a great communicator who also had excellent credibility on the subjects of his preaching; he would preach what he followed himself.** As presented earlier, all this was performed during the open season and the rainy season was allotted for general planning and the training and meditation of the monks.

Although the leaders and prophets of competing theologies would strongly oppose and disagree with Budh's teachings, **the masses**, in general, **would**, if they got convinced of his teachings, **convert to his faith without any conflict. This is because of the India's acceptance of the principle of clear distinction between Dharm and the freedom for the way of worship.** Budh was merely preaching his theology which fell in the basic concept of the freedom for the way of worship. So these conversions, not done by force, were not a threat to the Indian way of life and the tenets of law or the Dharm. Thus in many instances people who came to hear him converted to his faith en mass.

In general, **Budh's daily life was similar to his Order's ordinary monks**. He would rise early in the morning before sun rise, got ready, meditated, participated in a short discourse to his fellow monks or lay followers, and started to obtain food. He would make sure that nobody applied any pressure in receiving the food on the givers. He would welcome whatever was put in his bowl. He would walk on foot with his begging bowl in hand, and ate what he received. The food received was shared with rest of the Bhikshus. Thus, the food he and his monks ate was simple. Although meat was not banned, the edict was that no one would kill an animal for the purpose of feeding Bhikshus. **The Blessed One did not allow any distinction between the food he and his monks ate.** All what was received was first commingled for quality and then served to all. **This method ensured equality and fraternal feeling among all monks irrespective of their seniority and hierarchy in the Order.**

By this time, Budh had many wealthy disciples and people with positions in the society as his followers. He, however, made a rule that neither he nor any of his monks were allowed to accept costly gifts. The only things they would accept were simple cloths, shelter and food. If someone donated a piece of land then it was simply passed on to the order. Monks were not allowed to have any material possession of their own. Endowments to the *Sangh* were permitted in the form of garments for rain protection, bathing robes for the sisterhood, food for the transient Bhikshus and medicines for the sick and food for their attendants. All these rules were strictly followed. **Thus in Budh's Order, monks and his disciples were the people of discipline, sacrifice, desireless, service oriented and people of great character.**

There are many recorded events that illustrate Budh's character. The following two examples give a flavor of how he dealt with different social and human issues.

- The first examples is when two neighboring chieftains were on the verge of a war for the ownership of a disputed embankment that was very important for irrigation of fields on both sides of the Rohini River during an unusual drought period. When Budh was told that the armies on both sides were ready to fight, he went to them and asked them, that apart from the value of embankment for water rights, "does it possess any intrinsic value?" The answer from both sides was that it had no intrinsic value whatsoever. Then Budh posed another question, which was, "Does the blood of men, who will be killed in the battle, has lower value than a mound of dirt?" The answer from the men came in negative. Then Budh preached to them by saying that they should value the priceless human lives more than a mound of dirt which has no intrinsic value. The two chieftains realized their mistake and came to a peaceful friendly agreement.

- A second example is when after joining the Order, a merchant from Sunparant, whose residents were noted for their violent behavior, asked Budh's permission to convert his relatives to Budh's faith. Realizing this, Budh asked the merchant that, "if the people of Sunparant verbally abuse you, then what would be your response?" The merchant turned Bukshu replied that he would not respond to it in kind. Budh then asked if they strike or kill you, "what would you do?" The Bikshu's response was that he will not strike back. As far as killing is concerned, "death itself is no evil and many even try to escape from the vanities of life: I will take no steps to hasten or delay my departure." Hearing this Budh gave permission to this Bikshu to begin his missionary work (Gour,1929).

This way Budh spent time in traveling, spreading the word and preaching. When he was eighty years old he delegated his authority to his "true disciple" named Anand. Then he said, "From henceforth all my disciples, practicing their various duties, shall prove that my true Body the, Body of the Law, is everlasting and imperishable----all other things change, this changeth not-----." These were his last words and then he passed away.

Budh's various sayings are recorded in The Dhammapada (Dhamma means law, righteousness and pada means path or foot). There are various translated versions of Dhammapada available in English. A few of these sayings are presented below from over four hundred and fifty sayings documented in Dhammapada by Thomas Byrom (1976). The original document should be referenced for many other motivational sayings.

- We are what we think.
- Wakeful is one who never gives to desire.
- Look to your own faults and overlook the faults of others.
- Happiness or sorrow- whatever befalls you, walk on untouched, unattached.
- It is better to conquer yourself than to win a thousand battles. Then the victory is your.
- See yourself in others. Then whom can you hurt? What harm can you do?
- If you kill, lie, or steal, commit adultery, or drink, you dig up your own roots.
- Hold your tongue. Do not exalt yourself. But lighten the way for your words are sweet.
- Give thanks for what has been given to you, however little.
- The true master is "Possessing nothing and wanting nothing".

6.6 OVERVIEW AND BUDH'S GIFT TO HUMANITY

The earliest theological philosophy of the people residing in Indian subcontinent, during the period many thousands years before Budh, was recorded in **Vedic scriptures**. This philosophy recognized the Almighty as the supreme power but also personified various powers, such as, fire, sun and wind as gods who actually were described as having divine powers. As seers and sages contemplated and meditated they further realized the omnipotence, omnipresence and oneness (Monotheistic) nature of God. This was recorded in the scriptures called **Upnishads**. Upnishads expound that behind the diversities of the world there is one universal unity, the supreme Brahm. People may call it or worship it in different forms, e.g., Vishnu, Shiv, or other forms, but they all are one and the same. Thus, the Indian seers enunciated "the truth that the Supreme Being which is the universal cause and source of all existence is also the inner ruler of man".

At the same time, **many other theologies were being expounded, taught and discussed by other sages who belonged to various independent schools** of theologies that existed throughout the land. In accordance with the tenets of **Dharm, all these ways**, even if they may be different from ones belief, **were respected by the population**. Such was, in general, the theological environment of the Indian subcontinent prior to the birth of Budh.

Unlike in the previous periods when a person's occupation decided his class and social status, now different guilds wanted to protect their trade secrets and thus the society was now generally divided into casts based on their birth. All this caused a major resentment among many theological, social and political thinkers. The population, in general, was well fed from the standards of fifth and sixth century B. C. There was a large economic middle class; this resulted in producing a large number of social, political and theological thinkers.

It was under such theological, political and social environment that Gautam Budh was born in the year 563 B.C.

Sudhodhan, Gautam Budh's father was a chieftain king of a small state of Kapilvastu. When his pregnant wife Mahamaya was traveling to her parent's place, she gave birth to her son Sidharth Gautam on the full moon day of the month of Vesakh (April-May) in 563 B.C. Just seven days after Sidharth's birth his mother died and he was then raised by his step mother. When he became of school age he was taught language, arithmetic and Veds. As the prince grew older he preferred solitude and meditation instead of other fun activities, young adults of his age would normally get involved. Sidharth's father noticed his son's unusual activities and therefore got him married to Yasodhara. In due course their son Rahul was born.

Although Sidharth now had a happy family life and he had every worldly thing at his disposal, he began feeling as if something of great significance was missing in his life; this he felt was spiritual aspect of his life. While on his way outside his palace he saw **an old man** on the road. Seeing the worn out body of the man, he asked his charioteer about such a human condition. His charioteer replied that the old age is a decaying condition of humans and is an universal condition and all that is born must die. Next he saw a **sick man** who was in a real distressful condition. When he asked about this state he was told that such sickness is common to all in varying degrees. On a third occasion he saw a **dead body** being carried out for cremation. He was told that in the end we all have to face such fate. On the fourth instance he saw an **ascetic monk** who appeared calm, peaceful and full of self-control. **All this fired Sidharth's imagination and he immediately wanted to renounce the world and learn how to do good for humanity.** After initial resistance from his family, Budh left his family, friends and all his luxuries and became an ascetic with an aim to learn methods so that he could do good for humanity.

For the first six years of his renunciation and in search of truth, Sidharth visited various spiritual teachers and institutions of the time and learnt the theological principles and meditative techniques from them. He also discussed personally the rival doctrines with their exponents. Although Sidharth, by this time had learned and experienced different systems of philosophies and his mind was more calm and peaceful, still at the deepest level of his unconscious mind he felt that his mind was not totally pure.

At this time, Sidharth decided to practice self-mortification by practicing rigorous austerities (by fasting and other acts of self-denial) with five other seekers of salvation. As a result he was reduced to mere skeleton, "yet real wisdom still eluded him." With this experience Sidharth realized that either of the two extremes (i) a life led with all physical luxuries or (ii) a life led with physical torture and sever penance would not lead to Enlightenment. **"This realization turned him towards a middle path."** He then started taking food and decided to stay away from rigorous austerities. His five companions, who still believed that self-mortification was the way to Enlightenment, left him. He decided to continue his search alone.

Sidharth then, on a full moon day in the month of Vasakh (April-May), after taking a refreshing bath in the Niranjan River and then drinking milk, sat down below the shade of a Pipal tree. He sat there with the determination that he would not leave his seat till he attained Enlightenment. "He spent that night in deep meditation and rediscovered the long-lost technique of Vipassan." Sidharth Gautam became Gautam Budh (The wise, The Enlightened).

During this meditative state Bhudh with his pure and divine sight saw the **universal truth** as follows:
- **He saw that the living beings under the influence of evil actions pass through wretched worlds and those with good actions go toward in heaven.**
- **He then reflected that men's minds were ruled by desire. Desire arises where there is sensation, and sensation is produced by contact.**
- **Contact arises through six organs of the senses. These arise in the organism, where there is incipient consciousness, which arises from later impressions left by former actions, which again arise from ignorance.**
- **Thus ignorance is the root of the great trunk of pain. Therefore, ignorance is to be stopped by those who seek liberation.**

During the seven years of preparation and then during its last four weeks' of deep meditation, Budh had discovered the true path. He now began pondering if he should keep it to himself and enjoy the bliss by himself or if he should share it with others too. With the clear vision and determination in his mind Budh decided to disseminate his views and enlist disciples. For this, he turned to his first disciples who had earlier deserted him because they wanted to pursue the path of self-mortification to achieve "The Enlightenment". These five Bhikshus (a beggar who begs instructions for mind) were now seeking the path to Eternal Truth in the Holy city of Benares. So he departed to the Holy City of Benares. Then, Budh preached to his first five disciples in the following manner. He said that:

(A) The **noble truth of suffering** consists of (i) suffering in the birth, (ii) suffering in illness, (ii) suffering in decay, (iii) suffering in the object we dislike, (iv) suffering due to separation from our loved ones or things we love, and (v) suffering in the death. Thus, suffering is in clinging to these five existences.

(B) The **noble truth of the cessation of suffering** is complete abandoning every passion and desire.

(C) Finally, **Nirvan is achieved by following eight-fold path** that consists of: (i) Right Belief, (ii) Right Aspiration, (iii) Right Conduct, (iv) Right Speech, (v) Right Means of Livelihood, (vi) Right Memory, (vii) Right Endeavor, and (viii) Right Meditation.

After hearing this, the five Bhikshus were delighted and requested to be admitted in Bhudh's order which was duly accepted. Thus, these five were his first disciples and the first members of his Order.

As Bhudh preached his message, the number of his disciples grew fast. His message to his disciples was to travel from place to place for the welfare of the masses. He directed them **to preach the law, in spirit and in letter, so that people all over, irrespective of their background, become free from their bondage and achieve Eternal Bliss.** Budh trained, ordained and then sent his disciples in all directions to preach and make more converts. **His converts were from all casts, classes and occupations.** He told them **"Do not ask about descent, but ask about conduct."**

When he was asked by wealthy people, "**What was the use of riches**?" He replied, "**Charity**." When he was asked about cast, he said that **cast was occupational** as it had originally been; it has nothing to do with the birth of a person. It was not that only the kings, the nobles, the Brahmins and law abiding citizens but also the social deviants, such as, robbers were also impressed by Budh's piety.

Budh's teaching and preaching sessions were well planned and organized. Budh first would talk about the basic issues of life and death which everybody knew, and then he would bring up individual's and society's short-comings and finally **he would offer his well tried and practical solutions**. For most people in attendance this was enough and they would, if they agreed with his discourse, convert to his faith. Then there was time allotted for those who wanted to have one-on-one discussions with The Blessed One. **Budh was a great communicator who also had excellent credibility on the subjects of his preaching; he would preach what he followed himself.**

Budh spent time in traveling, spreading the word and preaching. When he was eighty years old he delegated his authority to his "true disciple" named Anand. Then he said, "From henceforth all my disciples, practicing their various duties, shall prove that my true Body, the Body of the Law, is everlasting and imperishable----all other things change, this changeth not-----." These were his last words and then he passed away.

Budh's various sayings are recorded in The Dhammapada (Dhamma means law, righteousness and pada means path or foot). A few of them are as follows:
- We are what we think.
- Wakeful is one who never gives to desire.
- Look to your own faults and overlook the faults of others.
- Happiness or sorrow- whatever befalls you, walk on untouched, unattached.
- It is better to conquer yourself than to win a thousand battles. Then the victory is your.

- See yourself in others. Then whom can you hurt? What harm can you do?
- If you kill, lie, or steal, commit adultery, or drink, you dig up your own roots.
- Hold your tongue. Do not exalt yourself. But lighten the way for your words are sweet.
- Give thanks for what has been given to you, however little.
- The true master is "Possessing nothing and wanting nothing".

REFERENCES

Byrom, Thomas, The Dhammapada, The Saying Of the Buddha, Bell Tower, New York1976.

Ch'en, Kenneth K.S., Budhism The Light Of Asia, Barron's Educational series, Inc.,1968.

Good News: New Testament and Psalms, cbs, Canadian Bible Society, Toronto, Canada1977.

Gour, Hari Singh, The Spirit of Buddhism, Lal Chand & Sons, and Rupa & Co. 1929.

Kaplan, Rabbi Arych, The Living Torah, A new Translation Based on traditional Jewish sources, Maznaim Publishing Corporation, New York, 1981.

Pickthall, Mohammed Marmaduke, The Glorious Qur'an, Translation, Tahrike Tarsile Qur'an, Inc, New York, 2000.

Prasad, R.C.,Tulsidasa's Shriramacharitamanasa (The Holy Lake of the Acts of Rama), Edited and Translated into Hindi and English, Motilal Banarsidass Publishers, Delhi, India,1999.

The General Libraries, The University of Texas at Austin, UT Libraries Online, 2003.

Vipasna Research Publications, Gotama the Budha: His life and His Teachings, Friend's Printery, Bombay, India, 1992.

Von Grunebaum, G.E., Classical Islam, A History 600-1258, translated by Katherine Watson, Barns & Noble Books, Aldine Publishing Company, 1970.

ABOUT THE AUTHOR

The author spent his early years in India's Himalayan region, where throughout the centuries, wise men have pondered and meditated about God and His creation. After receiving his bachelor's and master's degrees, over 35 years ago, he moved to America to pursue his graduate work and earned a Ph.D. degree.

The author enriched his experiences of living and interacting with people of various faiths in North America, by reading various scriptures, getting training on different theologies and visiting places of worship. He has also had the privilege of receiving sermons and/or blessings from leaders of various faiths including Pope John Paul II, Dali Lama, Shankaracharya and Swamis. Thinking and comparing the teachings of the Prophets, the author concluded that all Prophets had the same goal of leading the humanity to the righteous path as instructed to them by the Almighty God. Realization of all this, resulted in the conception and creation of this book.

Printed in the United States
99261LV00004B/150/A